How to Speak in Public

How to Speak in Public

ALEX MAIR

Hurtig Publishers
Edmonton

To Old Red, who's kept smiling through a lot
of chewy chicken and twice-told tales.

Hurtig Publishers Ltd.
10560 – 105 Street
Edmonton, Alberta
Canada T5H 2W7

Canadian Cataloguing in Publication Data
Mair, Alex.
      How to speak in public
ISBN 0-88830-275-4

1. Public speaking.   2. Oral communication.
I. Title.
PN4121.M34 1985   808.5'1   C85-091070-6

Edited by Nancy Marcotte
Illustrations by Graham Pilsworth
Design by Bob Young
Typeset by Attic Typesetting Inc.
Printed and bound in Canada
by the John Deyell Company

Contents

As the Christian said to the lion, "I
know why I'm nervous, but why are you nervous?"
And the lion said to the Christian, "Because
after dinner they want me to make a speech."

—Gordon Pinsent

CHAPTER 1

What is Public Speaking?

For most people, the thought of speaking in public conjures up one overwhelming image. The terrified public speaker is trapped at a head table in a smoke-filled room. The bar was open for an hour *before* dinner, the wine has been flowing freely *during* dinner, and the chairman for the evening has just told the after-dinner speaker that he needn't worry, that they will shut off the booze during his address. The speaker knows that this is not going to come as welcome news to the audience, which by this time sounds like a riot looking for a place to erupt.

The meal that the speaker tried to choke down is sitting there like a hot curling stone, just below and behind the middle of his necktie. His tongue has started to swell, his teeth have turned soft, and he knows that the instant he steps behind the lectern he's going to faint.

But the chairman calls for the attention of the audience. He explains that the entertainment for the evening will start as soon as the after-dinner speaker has finished and then proceeds to introduce said speaker, using three different pronunciations of his last name.

The poor speaker sits there trembling, wondering why he accepted the invitation in the first place, and looking around for a quiet spot where he can go and throw up.

While that is the image of the public speaker that comes quickly to mind, in reality there is far more to it. Public speaking is a form of communication. It is a way of getting your thoughts across to other people. There are many forms of communication, and in an era when we claim to have raised communication to an art form, you wonder whether the public speaker still fits in anywhere.

He fits in very well, because in this marvellous day and age in which we've done such great things with communication, the public speaker may be amongst the few people in the country who are doing any real communicating.

We sit down in the quiet of our living room to watch a televised hockey game. The game is being played in Moscow, halfway around the world, and what we are watching is called a "live" broadcast. There are differences in language, technology, time, and point of view, but do we take all of these into consideration when something happens to the picture? Not on your life! We become all upset if the colour balance between the reds and the blues isn't just right. The rest of it we take for granted.

At a time when we take for granted the transmission of a perfect colour-television picture from the other side of the world, we've lost the basic ability to communicate across the breakfast table, one person to another. We tend to forget that person-to-person conversation is just as important an aspect of public speaking as the trembling wretch who just dropped his notes all over the floor when he tripped on his way to the lectern.

Public speaking, no matter how you slice it, is communication one to another. The process may take place across the breakfast table, across the boardroom table, or across the front seat of an automobile as you try to convince someone that he or she really must buy this car if life is going to hold any charm through the years ahead.

Public speaking is convincing the students in a high school class that even at their age they might take a few minutes to find out what the poetry of Keats is all about. Keats's "On First Looking Into Chapman's Homer" is not, after all, a baseball story. Public speaking is convincing your young son that he really shouldn't stick crayons in his little sister's ear, and public speaking is telling the person facing you over the sugar bowl in the middle of the dining room table that you'd hate to think what life would have been like if the two of you hadn't decided to get married.

Granted, some kinds of public speaking are a little more

public than others, but it's all part of the same process. You have something that you want to say, a point of view that you want to express. You have an opinion about something, and you would like those around you to agree with that opinion and act accordingly. You may just want someone to really understand how you feel about a particular happening in your life. We all have these problems to face in the course of an average day, and in a century when we claim to have done all these exciting things with the process of communication, it's a little frightening to find how much difficulty we have when we try to share our personal message.

Whether you are dealing with a live audience numbering in the hundreds or a single client sitting across the desk from you, you are speaking in public and there are ways to make a better job of it. While the difficulties involved in speaking to the large audience may seem quite different from the problems connected with talking to just one person in a quiet room, there are a great many similarities shared by the two experiences. The factors that will make your exercise in public speaking a success with the large group are the same ones that will make it a success with your audience of one.

Remember, too, that there are very real rewards from all of this when you do make a success of it. Too much is said about the perils of public speaking but not enough is said about the rewards. Believe it or not, the rewards are there, even if you are the speaker down on his hands and knees gathering up the notes he dropped on his way to the lectern.

First of all, it's an honour to be asked to say a few words. It makes you feel good. Someone in this world has indicated that they are interested in what you have to say.

Not enough is said about the real thrill of doing a good job. That job may be explaining a technical point to a group of specialists, acting as an aid to digestion following a luncheon, convincing a couple that they should buy the house you have been showing them, or even getting your wife to agree that it would be a great idea to go back to the mountains for your summer vacation *again* this year.

It's a good feeling to have people sitting there paying attention to what you are saying. And if you can make them laugh and react and respond, your efforts have been all the more worthwhile. You are receiving the sincerest form of flattery—you have people *listening* to what you are saying.

The funny thing about speaking in public is that what you hear most are the horror stories. And the horror stories do stick in your mind, don't they?

It was a hot night in May at the old Macdonald Hotel in Edmonton. It was an international gathering of public health people, some four hundred and fifty of them, and I was their after-dinner speaker.

The problem started when the organizing committee, in their wisdom, put sixty-seven people at the head table. It wasn't easy. The hotel staff had to build a three-tiered platform to do it, but they managed. And then after dinner the master of ceremonies introduced the head table, all sixty-seven of them. And then he handed out life memberships to some of those attending, with a few appropriate words for each recipient. And then he handed out some *honorary* life memberships, again with a few appropriate words. By this time it was well after ten o'clock and they still hadn't quite got around to the after-dinner speaker. At this stage of the game the butterflies in my stomach were like the planes of the Strategic Air Command: some of them were airborne at all times.

I realized that they were getting close to my address, so I excused myself for a few minutes, explaining to the master of ceremonies that I was just making a nervous trip up the hall, not fleeing the country, and that I would be right back. I should mention that since it was such a hot night, I was wearing my one and only light-weight summer suit, which had been a help. I made my way to the men's room and, before heading back, proceeded to wash my hands.

You can say many things about the old Macdonald Hotel in Edmonton, one of which is that it had better water pressure than any other CN hotel west of Pugwash, Nova Scotia. The water went down the back of the washbasin, across the bottom, up the other side, and all over the front of my light-weight summer suit. If I'd been sitting down, I'd have been holding about a quart and a half of water in my lap. In three minutes I wasn't going to be sitting down, I was going to be standing up—in front of four hundred and fifty people.

Somehow I made it back to the head table, walking facing the wall every inch of the way. The lectern was going to be no help at all. It was held upright by a very narrow column of wood. I thought about snatching a bouquet of flowers from a vase on the head table and using it as a screen, but that would have looked a little suspect. The night's program was no help either. It was printed on a sheet of paper roughly the size of the six of clubs in a typical deck of cards.

So I did the only thing that came to mind. When I was introduced I stepped to the microphone, flung myself upon the mercy of the audience, and said:

"Funny thing happened on the way to the lectern."

CHAPTER 2
The Invitation

The invitation to say a few words can come from any direction. A well-organized program chairman for the local Home and School Association may call you five months in advance of the meeting he would like you to address. With that much lead time, you would be hard pressed to plead another engagement on the evening in question. A good program chairman knows that.

You may be asked to make a presentation at your company's annual sales meeting and you may be able to turn it into a brilliant opportunity to show senior management what an asset you are to the organization. Or it may be as simple as the suggestion over the telephone that you say a few words to that kid of yours when you get home from work tonight. Whatever the source and from whatever the direction, the invitation has been extended and you have accepted. Now the fun begins.

Keep in mind that somebody out there feels that you have something worthwhile to say. That has to be true or they wouldn't have asked you in the first place. Of course, there's always the outside chance that someone will call you at the last minute pleading with you to take the place of the speaker they *really* wanted, who has just been laid low with a nasty case of Rocky Mountain Spotted Fever. In that case, accept as gracefully as possible your status as a replacement and still keep in mind that somebody thinks you have something to say, even though they had someone else in mind who might presumably have said it better.

At this stage of the game there are a number of things you

can do that will make the whole experience a little less trying on your nervous system while making it more pleasant for all concerned.

It's a good idea to ask the individual extending the invitation to write you a letter confirming a few of the little details. These little details would include the date, the time, and the place. They may ask you to drop *them* a line confirming your acceptance. That's fair ball too. On a hot day in June, when someone asks you to address their meeting to be held shortly after the Thanksgiving weekend, you may make a note of it on the back of the flimsy copy of a gasoline credit card purchase and think you have everything under control. But it's amazing how the details can get away from you long before the end of August.

Having tied down the date, the time, and the place, it's always a good idea to spend a few minutes discussing your topic. *You* think you know what they've asked you to talk about, and *they* think they know what they've asked you to talk about, but it doesn't hurt to make sure you understand each other, which brings up another interesting point.

Different people view a topic in different ways. Ask about the makeup of the audience. The more you know about the people you'll be addressing, the better your chances of reaching them with your talk. If you were asked to say a few words about the way Canada's youth handle the English language and were told that your audience would be composed of high school English teachers, it's not so much that you would change what you had to say or alter your point of view, but you might touch up your *wording* a little.

It doesn't hurt to ask them how long you'll be expected to speak. A Presbyterian minister from Kilmarnock, in Scotland, was once asked to say a few words at the luncheon meeting of the Kilmarnock Rotary Club. During the meal, he asked the chairman how long they'd like him to talk. The chairman, without even lowering his knife and fork, said, "Talk as long as ye like, but the rest of us are awa' hame at two o'clock."

You'll find that very few people have a clear idea of time when they are talking about your speech, and you may have to lead them a little. If they are vague about the length of the talk, ask when they would like to have the whole meeting wrapped up. You will often find that they have a very definite idea as to what time they would like to clear the hall, and you can work backwards from that. Fifteen to twenty minutes is a rough guide for an address after a meal, whether it's a luncheon or a dinner. After half an hour you may notice the odd person in the audience taking off his wristwatch, shaking it, and then holding it up to his ear to see if it's still running. You may take that as editorial comment on the length of your address.

If it's a more structured program such as a sales meeting, a symposium of some sort, or your Home and School gathering, they will probably have a much clearer idea of the length of time you will have to work with, but always be prepared for surprises. If you are the first item on the program and the program starts on time, you have a reasonably good chance of being able to work with your entire allotted time. But if you are any farther down the list than the lead item, there are usually delays that will eat into your time. Even a luncheon can run later than expected. The dining room staff may dawdle over the servings. The president may have a few brief remarks that rival, in length if not in interest, the presentation of a federal budget. Someone may have an announcement to make and end up spending more time talking about the proposed bottle drive to raise funds for undernourished hamsters than you were given for your address.

For whatever reason, be prepared to find that you have less time than you expected. Trying to edit while on your feet is tricky at the best of times and disastrous at the worst. It's often a good idea to look over what you have to say with a view to thinking about what you can leave out if time gets a little tight. You will know that your time has been nibbled at before you stand up and it helps when you have already done a little advance thinking about shortening the thing if necessary.

Sometimes, in aid of efficiency and the best use of the time available, the chairman will turn you loose while the dining room staff is still serving dessert. An old friend of mine was invited to address the local Maritimers Association at their fall dinner meeting and decided to tell them ghost stories from Nova Scotia, his home province. He said later that it *might* have worked—had the waitresses not been gathering up dirty dishes all across the dining room as he tried to set the mood for his spooky yarns.

You certainly aren't going to resolve situations like this at the invitation stage, but by talking to the organizers and learning as much as you can about the function, you will often find that you can *anticipate* problems and prepare yourself accordingly.

It's always a good idea to find out whether your spouse is invited. If you are a husband, the tension involved in making an after-dinner address is not alleviated by the wife who sees you out the door, mentioning that she is about to make herself a peanut butter sandwich. The implication, of course, is that while you dine on pheasant under glass and fine wines, she'll be back home sweeping out the hearth and other related duties. And it doesn't help much when you are greeted at the door of the dining room by the program committee, who look stunned and then tell you that they *assumed* that you knew that your wife was invited, and that a place has been set for her at the head table.

During the invitation conversation, it's not a bad idea to make sure you know where to go when you arrive and if there is anyone in particular with whom you should check. A hotel can be a confusing place on a busy evening, and often there are two or three functions going on at the same time. You wouldn't want to spend twenty minutes detailing the fine art of trout-fly tying to a group of librarians who had gathered to hear a few well-chosen words on the problem of bag lunches in libraries, while the Fish and Game Association twiddled their thumbs in a room down the hall.

If you have been asked to talk about your holiday trip to Puerto Vallarta, it would certainly be a good idea to show a few of your 35mm slides. If you plan to do that, talk to someone about slide projectors. There's that awkward feeling that comes about when you walk in carrying your own Kodak Carousel and find one already set up on the card table in the middle of the room. And if your slide trays fit a particular projector, then take that particular projector with you. It's easier than scraping the egg of your face when you've accepted the offer of *their* projector and then find that *your* slide trays won't fit.

If you are planning to do anything in the audio-visual line, take two things with you: an extension cord and a spare bulb. The need for the spare bulb is obvious, and you'd be amazed at how often the nearest power outlet is half a day's march from where you want to set up your projector.

It may take someone a little time to find the janitor, who is the only person this side of Mazatlan who knows how to turn off the room lights. It may take your helper a few minutes to figure out how to run your projector or you may be faced with a short power failure. These are all possibilities which, with a little thought at the invitation stage, can be headed off at the pass.

While you are dealing with the details arising from the invitation, another problem may arise. There is an outside chance that the sound of your own voice may come to mind. It is quite likely that the way you sound to others has never ranked very highly on your list of priority concerns, but the phrase "ringing pear-shaped tones" may emerge from your subconscious. You may conclude that your tones are shaped more like a zucchini and wonder what steps could be taken to bring them into oratorical line.

The danger here is that you become overly concerned about the situation. It is true that dramatic and exciting things can be done to improve the sound of the human voice, but they don't happen overnight. If this is Tuesday and you've accepted an invitation to play your first game of golf next Saturday, signing up for lessons that start Thursday isn't going to do your backswing much good.

If it looks as though you will be doing more of this sort of thing, you may wish to pursue a training program. There's no point in practising bad speech habits. There are a number of books dealing with the topic of elocution and in most centres a number of courses are offered dealing with this form of training. A little investigation will reveal the program that meets your needs. But if this looks like a one-shot experience, you can quite possibly do more harm than good by fretting about your own eloquence. It could be one more tension-builder at a time when you don't need any more tension-builders. The people who extended the invitation asked you because of what you have to say, not how you sound.

However, even if this is a one-time-only experience, you want to do the best job possible. There are a number of simple exercises that help to loosen the lips and the tip of the tongue, and you might want to think about some of them while you assemble the pieces of your presentation. Many of them are designed to help your facial muscles relax, which in turn helps your voice to sound calm and relaxed. If you *sound* relaxed you are inclined to *feel* relaxed, and that's always a good thing for both you and your listeners.

Speech therapy and voice coaching are jobs for highly trained experts. But you may find that running through half a dozen "Peter Piper picked a peck of pickled peppers" helps to loosen the lips a little. I've also found that if I stretched my mouth into as wide a grin as possible, and then quickly pushed my lips forward as though someone had whispered that what I had just eaten was a raw oyster, the effect was a general relaxing of the muscles around the mouth. Deep breathing helps the tension situation as well. Blow all the old stale air out, and the fresh will find its own way back in. Repetition of any series of simple exercises adds to the benefit. There are all kinds of tongue twisters around, and they can be fun to play with. If you work with them over a period of time there is bound to be a beneficial effect, and you will gain a little more self-confidence.

You do have to pick your place of practice with a little care. If you are working at your lip exercises in the kitchen and your spouse comes in for a glass of milk, you may be suspected of dipping into the cooking sherry. And if you are driving along in your car and decide to tackle a tongue twister to while away the time until the light turns green, don't be surprised to find that the driver beside you waits until you have cleared the intersection before he starts to move. Wouldn't *you* give a five-car-length head start to any driver who talks to himself with that much animation when he's all alone in the car? While you are driving along the freeway you can work at your facial relaxing exercises in relative comfort and privacy. But if a driver passes you and then slows down to let you catch up so the kids in his back seat can have a look, don't be upset. At least you have given them an interesting topic of conversation for the next five miles.

Tongue twisters and relaxing exercises have a hidden benefit, too. If you are a little inclined to tense up at the thought of the invitation that you have accepted, they give you something to take your mind off your other muscles.

CHAPTER 3
Preparing the Thing

According to Funk and Wagnalls, the word "extemporaneous" is an adjective and means "1 uttered, performed or composed with little or no advance preparation. 2 prepared with regard to content but not read or memorized word for word." As far as your talk is concerned, extemporaneousness is like sainthood, an end devoutly to be pursued but fraught with difficulties in its achievement.

The goal you want to achieve is a comfortable rapport with your audience. This demands a delivery that is a natural presentation of your material with lots of eye contact with your listeners. You want to avoid the appearance of being a bundle of nerves reading from a prepared text. But how do you reach this lofty summit? Where do you start?

In actual fact, you may be tense, in a state of emotional turmoil, confused by your material, and convinced that you are about to clear the room faster than a fire drill. But you want to *appear* relaxed, composed, complete master of your subject, and in total command of your material. There *are* ways to achieve this seemingly-impossible goal.

It's not quite as flippant as it sounds to say that your first step should be to look at yourself in the mirror and tell yourself very bluntly that you've agreed to do this, and that even though you have grave misgivings about the wisdom of that decision, you are going to give it your best shot and do a good job.

Having done that, try to put that pesky part of the business out of your mind and settle down to deciding what you will say. You aren't going to make all the decisions about your material in one sitting. If you sit down behind a blank piece of paper, you are likely to find that you have a mind to match. But think about the job at hand while you are clearing the kitchen table, washing the car, working in the garden, or waxing the floor, and you will probably come up with a point or two that need mentioning. Write them down. As the great day gets closer, you will find that you have a fairly lengthy list of points. This is probably as good a time as any to apply the seat of your pants to the seat of a chair and impose some order on the whole thing.

Your first reaction will probably be one of dismay. Your list of points will seem so obvious that you will wonder why you accepted this invitation in the first place. Remind yourself again that somebody out there feels that you have something to say. That's why you were asked to speak. Things that are obvious to you may come as very fresh concepts to someone else.

Arrange these points in some sort of order and give a little thought to the way you will expand on them. You still have a few decisions to make, true, but at this point you have a bare-bones outline of the address you have been asked to present. The hard part is behind you. You have decided roughly what you want to say and now all you have to do is figure out the best way to say it. You have a lot of work ahead of you, but it can be interesting and it can be fun.

You have two rather difficult decisions to make at this stage. You must choose a way to get into your talk and you must decide how to get out of it. These two decisions may turn out to be the trickiest ones you will have to make.

Let's talk about this business of getting into it.

Let's make an imaginary jump ahead to your big night. We will assume that you have been introduced, that the introduction went fairly well, and that as you move to the lectern there is a wave of polite applause. Your immediate task is to give the audience a minute or two to settle down and become comfortable. There will be the rattling of coffee cups, the sorting out of cigarettes if there are smokers in the crowd, and a general shuffling of chairs as everyone twists around so that they can sit comfortably while they watch you talk. You are not going to say anything earth-shattering during this settling-down period. You may thank the chairman, you may make a comment or two on the introduction. You will probably say something about what an honour it is to be there and how happy you are to be talking to them. You may not feel that way right at that moment, but it's all right to say so whether or not it's true. These courtesies must be extended. Then it is time to get down to business.

Someone once started the rumour that all public addresses should start with a joke or two. This person is probably responsible for the rumour that lightning never strikes twice in the same place, that you can't teach an old dog new tricks, and that a bird in the hand is worth two in the bush but messier.

What you are trying to do at this point is to help your audience to feel comfortable with you and help yourself to feel comfortable with them. Making them laugh is the best way in the world to do that, but there are routes you can take other than the "telling of the joke" approach.

The speaker who moves to the lectern, clears his throat, and says, "Thank you, Mr. Chairman, for those kind remarks and that reminds me of a story," is in deep trouble.

A fellow called David Ogilvy, writing about the business of advertising on television, said in *Confessions of an Advertising Man* ([New York, Atheneum, 1963] 130) that the seven most deadly words in the world of television were, "And now, a word from our sponsor." Ogilvy claimed that those seven words were the signal to the viewer that he had at least two minutes to make a trip to the bathroom, cut back through the kitchen to build a peanut butter sandwich and open a cold beer, and get himself back in front of the set before the program started.

Ogilvy, a Scot who made a success in the advertising business on Madison Avenue, knows whereof he speaks. He went on to say that in magazine advertising you *don't* have your reader's attention and you have to catch it as they thumb through the magazine. In television, he claimed, the very opposite is true. You already have your viewer's attention and you don't want to lose it.

The same thing applies when you stand up to deliver your

address: you've got the attention of the audience and you don't want to lose it.

The six most deadly words in the world of public speaking are probably, "Which reminds me of a story." Take a tip from the world of successful television advertising. Tell them a story, but don't *tell* them you're telling them a story. Trick them into listening and they'll love you for it.

If this sounds just a little on the confusing side, let's take an example that has worked well for me in a variety of circumstances. As a rule, somewhere in my introduction will be a reference to the fact that I graduated in civil engineering. If it's not mentioned, I can always bring it up myself. After I've thanked the speaker, said hello to the audience in my own way, and given them a chance to settle down, I can mention rather casually that I feel very comfortable talking to them as a group. You can say that whether they are real estate agents, architects, physicians, or a high school graduating class. I will then go on to claim that the most difficult people in the world to talk to are engineers. We're looking at an example of a technique rather than a hard and fast rule. You, of course, may claim that members of your own occupation are the most difficult to address.

I might then mention that when I was an undergraduate at the University of Alberta away back in nineteen-never-mind, they had a rather strange rule that has never been explained, at least not to my satisfaction. Before we were allowed to graduate, we had to complete the first aid course offered by the St. John's Ambulance people. We questioned the need for all this, but it was our final year, we were approaching our last set of exams, and we were all very busy with what we deemed to be the main job at hand. We grumbled about this first aid thing, but we went along with it.

On the night of our first aid exam we discovered that we "almost engineers" were to be examined by members of the graduating class in medicine. The "almost doctors" were going to ask the questions, and I'm sure you'll know what I mean when I say that there was this deep, rich bond of affection between the engineering students and the medical students. I stood in line and listened as the fellow ahead of me took his seat opposite the "almost doctor."

"I see you're taking *civil* engineering," the med student said, "so I'll attempt to ask you a question related to your field." I wouldn't want to suggest that this "almost doctor" was in any way patronizing, but if you wanted to describe his attitude, you could say that humility was a trace element in his emotional makeup.

"Let's assume," he went on, "that you're in charge of a gravel-crushing operation and you've assigned a welder to carry out some repairs to the top of the crusher. As he's welding, the scaffold upon which he's standing suddenly gives way. As he falls, the welder passes the flame of the torch across the palm of his hand. As he goes down, he catches his forehead on a steel beam, opening a nasty gash just above the eyebrows. The force of that blow flipped his head back and he opened another nasty gash on the back of his head as he fell past another steel beam. As he dropped, the end of a broken timber opened still another nasty gash on the inside of his arm. He has landed on a pile of boulders beneath the crusher with one leg folded under him at a very unnatural angle and he's unconscious.

"Now tell me," said the "almost doctor," "what's the first thing you'd do?"

And my friend said, "Fix the scaffold."

While that may or may not be a typical engineer's response to the question, at least it leaves your audience with the feeling that while there may be *others* out there in the world who are too rigid in their thinking, that's certainly not a problem with this particular audience. The rapport with your audience has started to build, and the nice thing about it is that you were well into the story before they realized that it was "a story."

You can do the same sort of thing in a variety of ways. We all like to laugh at people who are so wrapped up in the job at hand that they lose all sense of perspective.

Peter Ustinov did a wonderful job on golfers in the course of a BBC television interview. He talked about the golfer who had been invited to play a round at the rather prestigious private club near where he lived. He was delighted, but he was also very nervous. At the first tee he managed to do everything wrong when he attempted to drive off. When he last saw his ball, it was disappearing over the top of a clump of trees bordering the freeway that ran past the club's property. He walked around the tee three times, breathing deeply as he went and muttering his ancient Hawaiian ritual chant of good luck. His second shot was down the middle, and the foursome headed off around the course.

When he came into the clubhouse after the round, the club president approached him and asked him if he was the gentleman who had managed to drift one over the trees in the direction of the freeway earlier in the afternoon. The visitor admitted that he was in fact the man and added that he hoped that there hadn't been any damage.

"As a matter of fact, that's what I wanted to talk to you about," said the president. "When your ball came down, it apparently struck an elderly cyclist on the forehead. The force of the blow caused the cyclist to lose control and he swerved to his left, into the path of a diesel semi-trailer truck approaching him from behind. The driver of the semi-trailer, in a rather vain attempt to avoid the accident, swerved into the path of a school bus driving in the next lane. The school bus driver slammed on *his* brakes, and, well, to cut a long story short, sir, the latest count is three dead, seven seriously injured, and they're still totalling the property damage."

The golfer covered his eyes in horror and said, "What am I going to do? What am I going to do?"

And the club president said, "Well, sir, you're going to have to hold your wrist a little more over the top, like this, you see...."

The importance of getting into your talk smoothly cannot be overestimated. It's during these few minutes that you build your association with your audience. It's that association that is going to make what you came to say the success that it should be and will be. It takes a little thought, but it can be done if you work at it during your preparation phase. And when it works, it's a delight to experience from either side of the lectern.

A few years ago, my wife and I attended a concert in what is called the Sun Dome, an auditorium in Sun City, just out of Phoenix, Arizona. The concert featured Joel Grey, the fellow who played the master of ceremonies in the movie *Cabaret*. There were thirty-five hundred people in the audience, most of them retired and either living or wintering in Arizona. This was what can safely be termed an "older crowd."

I was amazed when a young man walked out onto the stage and told us that it was his job to warm up the audience before the main concert began. He looked as though he would be barely old enough to have a paper route, and I wondered how a fellow that age was going to establish any kind of relationship with this older audience. But he did it with one story, and it was all over before his listeners realized that he had even started on a story.

He talked of his ninety-two-year-old friend, Fred, who called on his physician and told him that he was going to have to give up his regular game of golf. The physician was appalled. He told Fred that it was the regular exercise, the fresh air, the companionship, that was keeping him alive.

"Why in the world," asked the doctor, "would you want to give up something that's doing you so much good?"

"Well, doctor," said Fred, "at ninety-two I just can't see the ball anymore, and I think I had better call it quits."

But the doctor was a quick-thinking fellow and offered a solution. "Fred," he said, "I have another patient, a fellow called Herb, who's eighty-six. Herb loves to golf, has perfect eyesight, and would make a natural partner for you. Why don't I arrange a round for the two of you?"

And so it came to pass. Old Fred met Herb and they headed for the first tee the following Friday.

"I hear you've got pretty good eyesight," said Fred.

"Good eyesight?" roared Herbie. "I have eyes like an eagle. I can see for miles."

"All right," replied Fred. "You just keep your eyes on my drive and we'll get on with the game." Fred teed up his ball, went into his backswing, and got off a fairly good shot. He whirled around to Herb.

"Did you see where my ball went? Did you see where it went?"

And Herb snorted, "See where your ball went? Of course I saw where it went. I have eyes like an eagle. I can see for miles."

"Good," said Fred. "Where *did* my ball go?"

And Herb said, "I forget."

By the time the audience stopped laughing, the young man was in control. He had touched his audience with something to which they could relate. He poked a little gentle fun at one of their problems, and he made them laugh about it. And they liked him for that.

There's the basic idea. Now bend it to suit your individual needs. Tailor it to the group you are addressing. It's the idea that counts, not the actual story that you use to achieve your end. But keep in mind that your introductory story, to be most effective, should have some special relevance for the listeners.

Having got their attention, what do you do next? You turn to your list of points and get on about the job at hand. At this stage, of course, all of this is happening as you sit at your desk, but an ounce of preparation is going to be worth two bottles of antacid tablets on the big night.

You have arranged the things you want to talk about in the order you think best. Now consider the question of time. You have a fairly good idea at this stage as to the length of time the whole thing will take. Consider the attention span of your audience. Granted, the attention span will vary from one group to another, but don't try to make your audience work too long before you give them a break. A break isn't a fifteen-minute pause for a cup of coffee, it's a lighter piece of business worked into your talk. This brightener should relate to your subject matter in some way or cast a little light on it from a different point of view. If you choose your brighteners wisely, they'll poke a little fun at your topic and give your audience a rest so they'll be ready to get back to work.

Drop these brighteners in at intervals. Nobody wants to concentrate on a topic, any topic, for too long. The brighteners make it easier for your audience to stay with you, and they give you a breather as well. There's nothing quite like the sound of laughter from the floor to charge your personal batteries for another few minutes of running.

If you are at all apprehensive about the whole public speaking thing, why not write out what you want to say when you have reached this point in your preparation? It not only reassures you that your thoughts are lined up, but it will give you a good idea of the total time it will take you to cover your material.

Once you've got it down on paper, read it through *out loud*. You may be surprised to find that you will learn a great deal more about what you have on paper than the length of time it takes to read it. Some things that look perfectly harmless on a printed page can turn mean when you try to say them out loud. Don Harron, of Charlie Farquharson fame, tells of one of the earlier radio programs on which he appeared. It was called *Shhh, It's Music*. Don says that they finally had to change the name of the program because the host approached a state of nervous collapse every time he had to say it on air.

Words as harmless as "various nicks and notches" can take an evil form when you try to say them out loud, and watch for words like "tincture." They'll turn on you every time.

There was a morning when I tried to tell a story on live radio. I was talking about what the Wild West would have been like if they'd had drive-in restaurants. What I *attempted* to say was "Dodge City Chicken Shack." What I *did* say, like the last years in the life of Robert Burns, is best passed over lightly.

Writing things that are hard to say out loud can be done deliberately. The people who worked in CBC Winnipeg delight in telling the story of the night they did the chicken show in W. O. Mitchell's *Jake And The Kid* radio series. Mitchell deliberately used to write for one of the bit players lines that were very difficult to read. In one night's play, Mitchell had Jake and the Kid call on a neighbouring farmer, played by Mitchell's victim. In this episode, the Kid had been raising Leghorn chickens to further the war effort, and all of the chickens followed Jake and the Kid when they called on their neighbour. The chickens ran around the kitchen as the three of them tried to carry on a conversation. Mitchell had the character playing the farmer work himself into a rage, stand up and pound his fist down on the kitchen table, and shout, "You two get out of here right now. And take your whole clucking flock with you!"

Some things look quite innocent when you see them on a sheet of paper, but turn lethal when you try to lift them off the paper and say them aloud. A general rule is this: keep it simple. Peter Ustinov can use the words specious, spurious, and perquisites in the same sentence and not sound affected, but your average speaker is probably not as fortunate.

In the early years of this century a man called Bob Edwards was busy producing a newspaper that he called *The Calgary Eye Opener* and he said in his newspaper many things that are of interest and value to a speaker today. *The Wit & Wisdom Of Bob Edwards*, edited by Hugh A. Dempsey ([Edmonton, Hurtig, 1976] 112), records that Bob once said, "Don't tell all you know; keep a little for seed." That's not a bad thought to keep in mind when you are building your presentation.

In another collection, Dempsey brings us a unique Edwards quote that I have often used with great success to solve the second of the terrible two problems, the closing.

When you are finishing up, it is always better to finish with a bang rather than a whimper. There is something awkward about finishing your address and realizing that you are the only one in the place who knows that you are through. When you are putting the pieces of your talk together, spend a little time considering the best way to wind it up, making sure that your audience *knows* that you are all done. That is the stage I was at when I first turned to *The Best of Bob Edwards*, also edited by Hugh Dempsey ([Edmonton, Hurtig, 1975] 60).

When I have brought everything together at the end of an address, I have found it very effective to say that I would like to quote a few lines by the editor of the old *Calgary Eye Opener*, the late Bob Edwards. Bob said in so few words, I explain, what I have been trying to say in so many. Bob wrote a prayer on one occasion, a prayer that came out this way:

Lord, let me keep a straight way in the path of honour—and a straight face in the presence of solemn asses. Let me not truckle to the high, nor bulldoze the low; let me frolic with the jack and the joker and win the game. Lead me unto Truth and Beauty—and tell me her name. Keep me sane, but not too sane. Let me not take the world or myself too seriously, and grant more people to laugh with and fewer to laugh at. Let me condemn no man because of his grammar and no woman on account of her morals, neither being responsible for either. Preserve my sense of humour and of values and proportions. Let me be healthy while I live, but not live too long. Which is about all for today, Lord. Amen. When you get to the Amen, they *know* you're done.

CHAPTER 4
Delivering the Goods

Somebody once said that there were only three basic rules to public speaking: stand up, speak up, and shut up. Oh, would that it were that simple!

It's likely that at this stage of the game you are wondering how you are going to make out when it comes to delivering your address. A legitimate concern, of course, but not one that should in any way hinder the digestion of your last meal.

In those marvellous recesses of your mind where all things are happy, where your stomach doesn't bulge, you are never overdrawn at the bank, and you drive a Rolls Royce to the supermarket, you can hear yourself delivering your carefully-crafted prose. And you sound like Lorne Greene or Ingrid Bergman, don't you? But back in the real world you know that you *don't* sound like that. You would like to have a voice so rich and smooth you could pour it on a pancake, but you haven't, so don't fight it. Work with the voice that you've got and things will be just fine.

If you want a little real encouragement, track down someone who has a collection of old records and borrow a few of them. I'm not talking about just any records but some by the stand-up comedians who were great names when they first broke into the recording business and still are great names today. Try to find the Warner Bros. recording of *The Button-Down Mind of Bob Newhart* (#1379) or Bill Cosby's *Why Is There Air?* (#1606) by the same recording company. If you can find one of these classics, sit down in a dark room, put the record on the turntable, and just listen to it with no distractions. Bob Newhart's voice and delivery are about as far removed from Lorne Greene's as you are going to get, but nobody has ever suggested that Newhart's voice is unpleasant. You like it because it is so natural that you hardly even notice the hesitant stammer that has become an integral part of his style. If you can't get hold of an old Newhart record, listen to him talking on any of his television shows. His technique is still the same and it still works. The same thing will work for you if you just relax, stay natural, and talk in your own way. Remember, we are not discussing what you have down on paper at this point, just the way you are going to deliver it.

On the subject of being natural, let's take a minute to consider Bill Cosby. Any man who can sit down on a front porch and eat chocolate pudding with a group of small children and have it turn into a successful television commercial is doing something right. He's being natural and that's why it's so effective, whether he's flogging pop or pudding.

Some of those early Cosby albums are classic examples of the art of the monologue. And what did he talk about? He talked about the kids with whom he'd grown up, about their neighbourhood, about going to school, about getting his tonsils out, and about borrowing his dad's car. He even refers to his childhood friends in the natural way that a child would. He talks about Weird Harold and Fat Albert. He's made Fat Albert so famous they've named a light bulb after him.

Don't be afraid to use a few gestures while you are talking. Nobody says you have to stand there with your hands gripping the sides of the lectern as though you were holding the whole room steady. Move your hands and arms a little. Glance around your audience and let that physical animation carry over into your voice, because it will.

There's an old childhood game that works well in the training of announcers for the broadcasting industry. Give someone a magazine and ask him to read aloud a paragraph from one of the stories, and then to read it again. The trick is that the reader must have his back turned to you so that you can't see his face, and he must give the paragraph one reading while smiling and one reading while frowning. He is not allowed to tell you which reading is which.

The surprising thing is that he doesn't have to tell you. You know within the first five or ten words which reading is done with the smile and which with the frown. You won't believe this until you try it for yourself, but it really works.

Rich Little, probably one of the world's best impersonators, makes an interesting point when talking about his work. He says that when he is developing the impersonation of a character, any character, he tries to master the movements and gestures before he ever tries to imitate the voice. Watch him the next time he does his impersonations on television. The voices are incredibly accurate impersonations, but the gestures are clearly identifiable too. It's interesting to know that Rich Little learns to *move* like somebody before he tries to *sound* like them.

If you want to sound poised, relaxed, and sure of yourself at the lectern, give some thought to the way you would move if you really *were* poised, relaxed, and sure of yourself at the lectern. Work on the movements a little and see what interesting things happen to your delivery. Then try to tense up, put a frown on your face, and try again. You will be amazed at the difference it can make in the way your material is lifted off the printed page.

You can personalize your delivery by glancing around at your audience and talking to someone in the group while looking them right in the eye. The room may be full of people, but you are actually just talking to them one at a time. Watch that face for reaction. Look that person in the eye as you drop in a brightener and see that face light up in response.

Of course it doesn't always work out that way. It was a February night in Yellowknife, and you can imagine what it's like in February in the Northwest Territories. The event was the annual meeting of the Yellowknife Chamber of Commerce. I was the after-dinner speaker and it certainly wasn't cold inside that night. The audience was warm, comfortable, and responsive. I picked out one fellow in the audience and began to watch him for reaction as I got into the thing. It was a disaster.

The harder I tried, the more impassive the face became. There was no expression. A blank. The blank changed to bland indifference when he got out his Zippo lighter and cleaned the flint wheel with his pocket knife, notch by notch.

Quite by accident later in the evening I learned that the fellow was deaf, that the battery in his hearing aid had conked out very early in the proceedings, and that he hadn't brought a spare battery with him.

I first ran into this business of breakdown in communication a long time ago when I was teaching Sunday School. There comes a time when no matter how thoroughly and skillfully you prepare your material or how hard you try, you are not going to get through to your audience. I remember the Sunday morning I had that lesson driven home with great force.

I was superintendent of the Primary Department. On a good Sunday (or a bad one, depending on your point of view) we could have as many as a hundred and thirty kids in attendance. As superintendent, part of my job was to get them settled down. We sang a few hymns, we took up a collection, and then I told them a story that set them up for the classroom portion of their Sunday morning. When I had finished my contribution, the kids would break into groups of ten or twelve and with their individual teachers they would pursue the topic that I had so carefully placed before them in the open session.

On the Sunday in question we were dealing with the story of Nehemiah. He was the fellow who climbed onto his camel at Susa and rode four hundred miles to the City of Jerusalem. When he arrived he was horrified to find that the walls around the city had all crumbled and broken down. With the walls in disrepair, the people of Jerusalem had slumped into a state of lethargy and economic decline. It was Nehemiah who organized the people of Jerusalem into work parties. He had some make building blocks and others cart away the debris of the old wall. Still others he organized into construction crews that rebuilt the wall around Jerusalem. When he climbed back onto his camel to go home to Susa, the new wall was finished, the people had perked up, and the City of Jerusalem was a happy, vibrant place in which to live and work once again.

When I had finished my portion of that Sunday's session, I thought that if we had ever done a thorough job on a Bible story, this was it. The teachers had all been primed and had special projects planned to help illustrate the story as they examined it in their smaller groups.

When the children headed for their classrooms that morning, there was a sense of excitement that I could feel. But when they were singing the last hymn upstairs and our classes were finishing downstairs, one of the Grade Two teachers came over to me with a grin and said that he was sorry, but it just hadn't worked. The boys in his class were convinced that this man's name wasn't Nehemiah at all, but that he was a short building contractor whose name was Knee-High Meyer.

And while it's a long way from a Sunday School room to the Broadway stage, you can learn a lesson in public speaking from the stage end of the spectrum as well. When playwright Joseph Stein, composer Jerry Bock, and lyricist Sheldon Harnick took the stories of Sholom Aleichem and turned them into the musical called *Fiddler on the Roof*, they chose Zero Mostel to play the part of Tevye when the work opened on the London stage. A friend of ours saw Mostel play that part in London and came home to tell us that one of the highlights of the evening was Zero Mostel standing, stage centre, and belting out the lyrics to the song "If I Were A Rich Man" as only Mostel can belt.

When Norman Jewison made *Fiddler on the Roof* into a film (Mirisch/United Artists, 1971), our friend went to see the motion picture version of the play he had seen performed live on the London stage. This time the part of Tevye was played by Topol. Topol took the same lyrics and did them *his* way. Topol seemed to feel that "If I Were A Rich Man" was really a conversation between a man and his God, and you don't yell when you are talking to God. If you saw the film you may remember when Topol very quietly began by saying:

As the Good Book says, "Heal us, O Lord, and we shall be healed." In other words, send us the cure, we've got the sickness already. I'm not really complaining—after all, with Your help, I'm starving to death. You made many, many poor people. I realize, of course, that it's no shame to be poor, but it's no great honor either. So what would have been so terrible if I had a small fortune?

And then, more to himself than to his God, Topol begins the song as he half-whispers, "If I were a rich man...."

Our friend who had seen both versions came away saying that he had no idea that delivery could make such a tremendous difference to the perception of exactly the same set of words. Topol's was natural, it had feeling, and it worked.

Another nice example of keeping something simple and natural can be found in the lyrics that Alan Jay Lerner wrote for *My Fair Lady* (Warner, 1964). Eliza Doolittle sings to herself the rather haunting lyrics to "Wouldn't It Be Loverly." And what does Eliza want to make her world loverly? All she wants is a room somewhere, far away from the cold night air. Think about the other things she'd like to smooth out her life. Lots of coal making lots of heat, lots of chocolate for her to eat. Oh, wouldn't it be loverly.

Your delivery can be effective too if you can achieve the same simplicity and naturalness in the preparation of your material and the presentation of it when you stand up to speak. Write it all out, certainly. But remember that when you are making your delivery, it isn't natural to bow your head and *read* the whole thing. It's natural to look up and talk *to* your audience. You'll find that this can happen if you've prepared your remarks with the real *you* built in.

Don't try to sound like someone else when you put it down on paper and you won't have any trouble sounding like yourself when you try to lift it off the paper.

You'll find after the first few minutes that, because what you put down on paper is what you naturally think and feel, you don't have to refer to the printed page before you to make the points with your audience. You'll be able to look *at* and talk *to* them, knowing that you can always glance down and refresh your memory if the familiar words don't come quickly to mind.

You may become so comfortable with your material that you would like to simplify your preparations one step farther. You may discover that all you need are one or two words to remind you of the point or the story that comes up next. If that begins to happen, get yourself a few cardboard recipe cards and go through your talk, summarizing each paragraph with a one- or two-word clue that you can write down with a felt marker on your cards.

If things are really working well, a glance down at the large friendly words on your recipe cards will prepare you to look your audience in the eye and hold their attention until you are ready to hit them with your next point.

If you decide to work with that system when the big event rolls around, let me pass on a small lesson that was learned the hard way. When you have your cards all filled out and arranged in order, pick up your flow pen again and *number* the cards in the upper right-hand corner. There was the night that I headed for the lectern, recipe cards flexed a little in my right hand the way a Mississippi riverboat gambler would flex a deck of cards. Then, zing, and there were cards all over the floor. There was Joe Cool, down on his hands and knees with the chairman for the evening, a very charming lady, helping him to pick up all the cards while the audience wondered where everyone had gone all of a sudden.

If you still feel a little nervous about how an audience is going to receive what you are planning to say, think about Thomas Carlyle's comment about the poems of Robert Burns.

Carlyle wrote an essay on Burns, and while he was talking about the Scots poet he had a word or two of rather sound advice for anyone who is going to attempt to speak in public. Carlyle put it this way:

> Let a man speak forth with genuine earnestness and thought, the emotion, the actual condition of his own heart, and other men, so strangely are we all knit together by the tie of sympathy, must and will give heed to him. In culture, in extent of view, we may stand above the speaker or below him; but in either case, his words, if they are earnest and sincere, will find some response within us. For in spite of all casual varieties in outward rank or inward, as face answers to face, so does the heart of man to man. (*Selected Writings* [Harmondsworth, England, Penguin, 1971] 44)

CHAPTER 5

In the Beginning was Style

No public speaker has ever intentionally stood up before his audience, cleared his throat, and said, "If youse'll just pay attention, there's something I'd like to say."

Winston Churchill worked with the same language as the politician who put you to sleep at the meeting you attended before the last civic election, and Beethoven was working with the same musical notes as Stompin' Tom Connors. The sound of Churchill's oratory and the sounds of Beethoven's music must owe their worth to something beyond the basic building blocks from which they were constructed. Perhaps it's an over-simplification, but consider for a while the possibility that this "something" could be described with just one word—style.

If you were to describe the verbal delivery of a politician such as Teddy Kennedy, you could say that he has a distinctive style. That style comes from more than his accent; it comes from the way he uses the language. I hadn't thought much about the Kennedy style until I read a piece that William Reel wrote for the *New York Daily News* on November 21, 1979. Reel said:

I get the feeling that if you asked Teddy Kennedy for the right time, he would reply that while he has a position on what time it is, and always has had a position on what time it is, and has never shrunk from facing the very delicate issue of what time it is, still, he wants to weigh all the considerations regarding the different facets of what time it is, and discuss the parameters with his advisers and then respond to the question at some appropriate point in time.

I was so impressed with the way that the piece *sounded* like Ted Kennedy that I used it in an address shortly after it appeared in print. To my amazement, a member of the audience came up to me later in the evening and said that I didn't have to use a created quote like that because the real thing was even funnier. To prove his point he gave me a copy of a Kennedy statement that had appeared in *Time* magazine on February 11, 1980. It seems that Senator Kennedy had been asked how he hoped to deal with the Soviet Union while avoiding a resumption of the cold war.

According to *Time*, the *first sentence* of Kennedy's reply was:

> Well, I think we need a foreign policy which is tied to our national security interests, which are tied to intelligent interests for the United States, that are tied to energy interests, which are tied to a sound economy here in the United States and an energy policy that is going to free us from heavy independence to the Persian Gulf countries and to OPEC, which is strongly, which has the strength and the support of the American people, and which is predictable and certain, which has a down side to it in terms of disincentives to the Soviet Union for actions which are contrary to the standard of both international behavior and also has incentives to the Soviet Union to try to work in ways that can at least some, uh, create at least a world which is going to be freer from, uh, the nuclear nightmare which hangs over the world.

Somebody once said that humorists have the same problem as the world's oldest profession. It's not the honest competition that gets to you, it's all the amateurs going around doing it for nothing.

Very learned books have been written on the subject of style in writing. One of the better ones (and not because with its seventy-one pages it's the shortest) is *The Elements of Style* by William Strunk Jr. and E. B. White. This little book was originally written by Professor Strunk before 1920 but was revised by White, who also added a new chapter in 1957. It is interesting to note that Strunk's version probably ran to some fifty pages. White, when he added the fifth chapter, called "An Approach to Style," increased the number of pages by almost half. The four chapters written by Strunk dealt essentially with questions of grammar and the use of the language. White's addition takes the firm rules laid down in the first four chapters and goes on to explore the question of style in its broader meaning.

I've always found it significant that when he wrote the introduction for the revised edition, White referred to his addition to the book and said, "This chapter...is addressed particularly to those who feel that English prose composition is not only a necessary skill but a sensible pursuit as well—a way to spend one's days." (3d ed. [New York, Macmillan, 1972] xii) I've always felt that White was talking about the spoken word as well as the written word when he said that.

We have done something mysterious to the language over the past few years. It's not so much that we use fifty words when five would do, but that we all try so hard to sound sophisticated that when we come across something that has been written or spoken with natural simplicity and clarity, we are refreshed and delighted. Richard Reeves, writing in the *New Yorker* magazine for April 5, 1982, quotes from *The New Age*:

Now that living together out of wedlock has become so common, many American institutions have been trying to come up with words that can be used in place of such terms as "husband," or "wife," or "married couple." The Ford Foundation has replaced the word "spouse" with "meaningful associate" and the National Academy of Sciences, instead of saying "husband" or "wife," now employs the term "special friend." One maternity hospital in Washington, D.C., asks expectant mothers not for the father's name, but for the identity of the "significant other person."

Speak with simplicity, clarity, and naturalness, and you will be as welcome as the birds in spring.

Max Beerbohm said of radio broadcasting that the sound was always important to him, that he laid great emphasis on the acoustics of prose, and that in radio broadcasting these were paramount.

We lost a lot of style in the spoken word when we put the King James version of the Bible on the shelf. "Consider the lilies of the field, how they grow. They toil not, neither do they spin" has become "Look at all them yellow flowers that don't do nothing but sit there and shed pollen."

Because there are words that have in themselves an interesting sound, you can breathe style into your spoken words through the judicious choice of your words. There are words that roll off the tongue, words like aspic, vicissitudes, the path of righteousness, zinnias, firkin, and stephanosis.

There are ways to put things into your prose that lift the basic observation out of the ordinary and give it life and vivacity.

Loading kids into a car is like stringing beads with no knot on the end of the cord.

Begin a story the way you pick up a wet puppy, just a little ahead of the middle.

The trouble with being a good sport is that you have to lose to prove it.

So narrow-minded he could look through a keyhole with both eyes at the same time.

Or as Richard Needham put it in the Toronto *Globe and Mail*, "So you don't live up to other people's expectations? Cheer up! Neither does God."

An English professor showed me an essay that had been submitted to him while he was still teaching at the University of Southern California. The student was trying so hard to produce thc definitive work on the life and times of Johann Sebastian Bach that he lost sight of his own horizon. The student began the essay by saying, "Johann Sebastian Bach had twenty-three children and practised on an old spinster he kept hidden in the attic."

In this day and age you can take what G. K. Chesterton had to say about Christianity and expand it to include the spoken word. The revised version would run, "Christianity and simplicity have never been tried and found wanting. They've been found difficult and not tried."

Pursue simplicity and you have taken the first step on the road to style.

The best advice I've ever heard on the subject of English composition came not from a writer but from a photographer. He was the senior instructor in a two-year photography course at an institute of technology. Shortly after the start of the first year, this fellow would book a school bus and load the entire first year class into it and take them on a field trip to a national park nearby. Each student came equipped with a camera loaded with black and white film and instructions to photograph whatever interested him or her.

My friend claimed that year after year he found that the student who roared out of the bus and began looking for the picture that was going to make the next cover of a national magazine was invariably the student who failed the exercise. The student who *succeeded*, he claimed, was the one who never wandered more than twenty paces from the door of the bus. It would be the student who knelt down and took a picture of a dandelion going to seed or looked up and photographed a drop of moisture on the tip of a leaf who produced the print that deserved to be remembered.

The instructor claimed that the successful photographer is the one who climbs a step ladder and takes his picture looking down, or who gets down on his stomach on the ground and shoots looking up. The successful photographer sees the same world that the rest of us see, but he steps to one side to take his picture, or he climbs up and looks down. He views the world from a slightly different angle. My friend used to say that the surest indication of a good photograph is when someone looks at it and says, "You know, I've seen that a thousand times before, but I have never looked at it from quite that angle."

The same thing can be said of the written word or the spoken word. If you can deliver an address and have someone come up to you when you are through and tell you that they had never thought about the subject from that point of view before, you know you were on the right track.

Achieve this fresh perspective and you have moved another step along the path towards style.

For thrift and economical use of the language, there are some classic examples to be found in the work of Dorothy Parker. She reviewed a book on one occasion with two short sentences. "This is not a novel to be tossed aside lightly. It should be thrown with great force." (Quoted by Robert E. Drennan in *Wit's End* [London, Leslie Frewin, 1973] 116)

There are only seventeen words in that review, but you are in no doubt as to how Mrs. Parker felt about the book.

Leonard Lyons once asked Dorothy Parker to describe her Bucks County farm in two words, to which she replied, "Want it?" (ibid., 122)

These two brief examples take on new meaning when you remember that this was the same Dorothy Parker who said, "Wit has truth in it; wise-cracking is simply calisthenics with words." (ibid., 124)

Put wit in your work and you've come another giant step along your path to style.

Looking back at this point, we have worked our way through the preparation of the address, spent a little time considering the best way to deliver it, and considered some elements of style that can go into the spoken word. We may even have left the suggestion that it's the *style* that will catch the interest of your audience and hold that interest while you say what you have to say.

It doesn't really matter how important your topic might be, how well documented your case, or how strong your sales pitch. If your audience isn't listening, you are fighting an uphill battle.

You might even be justified in wondering whether it was really worthwhile to *try* to get people to listen. Can you really break through the mental blocks and barriers that people have built around their favourite points of view? Or are they still going to sit there rearranging their prejudices and calling it thinking?

Just about everyone has, at one time or another, stood around a piano and contributed what they could to the singing of that old favourite, "You Take the High Road and I'll Take the Low Road," sometimes known as "Loch Lomond." Not everyone has heard the story behind the story of the lyrics of that song. It tells the story of two Scottish soldiers who were captured by the English and imprisoned at Carlisle, just south of the border. The English tried the two, found them guilty, and sentenced one of them to death the following morning. The other soldier, in a nice example of applied psychological warfare, was to be set free. Then they told the two soldiers which one was to be executed the next day and which one was to be set free. Then they locked the two of them up in the same cell to spend their last night together.

In Scots mythology there are two road systems. There is the high road, which runs from one town to another and is taken by the traveller. There is also the low road, the road of the spirit.

The lyrics to that song are sung by the soldier who knows he is to die in the morning, and he sings them to his fellow prisoner:

You take the high road, and I'll take the low road
And I'll be in Scotland before you
Though me and my true love will never meet again
On the bonnie, bonnie banks of Loch Lomond.

So you see, it *can* make a difference when you get someone to listen to the story behind the story that they think they've heard a hundred times before.

CHAPTER 6

What's So Funny About Humour?

When you sit down to work at it, you suddenly realize that humour is a very serious business.

Humour is an invaluable tool to the public speaker. Through the effective use of humour, the speaker can loosen up the people in the audience, win them over to his side, and help them to relax for a few seconds in the course of an otherwise serious talk. If he can close with something light and leave them with smiles on their faces, they'll remember him fondly for it.

The instant we sit down and try to analyze what is funny and why, we run into trouble. A funny story, if you have to explain it, ceases to be funny.

The New Yorker a few years back ran a cartoon that has turned out to be somewhat of a test of the reader's sense of humour. The cartoon itself was a rectangle of solid black ink. There was nothing else in the cartoon, just that rectangle of black. The caption read, "Hello Coast Guard? This is Johnson at the lighthouse."

There were people who roared with delight when they saw the cartoon, and there were those who held it up to the light to see if there was something they hadn't seen. No two people view humour in exactly the same way, but don't ever suggest to anyone that they don't have a sense of humour. We all feel that we have a keen sense of humour. It's just that we laugh at different things.

Humour, in some ways, is like night vision. Fighter pilots in World War II were taught that if they were trying to see something in the dark they were never to look right at it.

They were to look all around it, and by doing that they gained an awareness of what was there. Like an object in the dark, humour, if looked at directly, can't be seen. But if we look all around it we may gain an awareness of what is funny.

I remember going to see a movie starring Cary Grant, and I found it to be so funny that I went back twice to see it over again. It was billed as a "humorous mystery drama" by Russel Crouse and Howard Lindsay, and it ran for 1444 performances on Broadway. The plot deals with two elderly maiden ladies who lure lonely old men into their home on the pretext of renting them a room, then poison them with arsenic added to a glass of their homemade wine. The bodies are then buried in the cellar with the aid of a demented nephew. Hardly the stuff of humour, surely, but funny enough to run for 1444 performances on Broadway and when it was made into a movie, funny enough to cause me to see it three times. It was called *Arsenic and Old Lace*.

But if the plot wasn't funny, what was there to laugh at? It was the *treatment* that was funny, not the *topic*. Therein lies a great lesson.

Look at the works of Neil Simon, a man who is held to be one of the funniest playwrights that you'll find. Simon's *The Odd Couple* tells the story of two men who have been thrown out of their homes by their wives, one because he was such a slob that his wife couldn't stand him, the other because he was so fastidious that he was driving the rest of the family out of their minds. These two opposites, rejects in many ways, and the way they learn to cope with each other, are the basis of the play. A sad story, really, but with the Simon treatment it becomes a comic delight that makes us all laugh.

Take any Neil Simon play and look at the story line and you will realize that in each case the humour comes not from the topic but from the treatment. They are all sad stories. It's the way they are handled that makes us laugh.

Most people will deliberately go out and look for something funny when they want to lighten an address. Perhaps what they should be doing is considering their topic and looking for something funny in that. The writers of the incredibly successful television series *M*A*S*H* have had their work described as comedy, but it was the humorous treatment of a tragic subject that enabled us to look upon each episode as a comedy.

You can find something funny in the law, in politics, or in the home. Erma Bombeck has been delighting newspaper readers for years with her daily glimpses behind the domestic scene. Each item deals with a simple, down-to-earth aspect of family living. In themselves the Bombeck topics aren't what you would call funny, but by the time the Bombeck treatment has been applied they become a daily delight.

Take your topic, give it the treatment that will enable the listener to look at it in a different way, and with luck you will catch him by surprise. Make all that happen and you are well on the way to making humour work for you.

If the first trick of humour is to be found in the treatment, surely the second one is based on surprising your listener. You don't laugh at the story whose punch line you figured out three minutes earlier. You laugh at the story that catches you completely by surprise, and you don't find anything added to the element of surprise if you've been signalled in advance that you were about to hear a funny story.

Another fundamental aspect of working in a bit of humour is that you must be very comfortable with it. It must be the sort of story that *you* feel natural in telling. It may seem a little trite, but don't tell your audience a story that you wouldn't tell your mother. Any discomfort that *you* feel will be picked up by your audience, and then you are all uncomfortable.

For fourteen years we shared our house with a crossbred German shepherd dog that we called Lady. We often said that she was just like a member of the family, but we were very careful to avoid saying *which* member of the family.

As Lady grew older and a little more arthritic, one of her daily rituals was an evening walk around the block before she settled down for the night. There was one spring evening when the dog and I headed out for that last whiff of fresh air. It had rained, and there were puddles of water all over the place. The dog cut down through one puddle, up through a flower bed, back through another puddle, and then on to another flower bed. I remember raising my voice in frustration and calling, "Lady, if you wouldn't put your big flat feet in the middle of every puddle in the neighbourhood, you wouldn't be such a mess when you got home."

The dog didn't pay any attention to me at all, but the middle-aged woman walking just in *front* of the dog whirled around, and...well, I could have talked all night and she wouldn't have been convinced that I wasn't offering an editorial comment about her.

When you're using humour, watch it! Humour can turn into a vicious weapon, and often the storyteller is the last one to realize it. Somebody out there may be hurt, even though no hurt was intended. We are all sensitive about something, and what may be an honest attempt on your part to take a light look at something could be viewed as an attack by someone on the other side of the lectern.

I once talked to a group of high school students on the subject of humour. I was writing a daily humour column for a newspaper at the time. During the question-and-answer period, one of the students asked me if I was bothered by the feeling of power. I didn't understand, and said so. The student very quickly said, "When you're using humour, you can hold some*one* or some*thing* up to ridicule and destroy it."

I was once appointed a member of a two-person committee to buy a gift for a senior administrator down at the office, and it wasn't an easy job. He was an intensely practical man, and what he would have liked was a new set of tips for his welding torch. The other member of the committee, a charming young lady, felt that something along the lines of an Eskimo carving was the sort of thing we were really looking for. The situation was further aggravated by the fact that the president had told me privately that he didn't want an excessively expensive gift from any one group since there were to be a number of presentations. The top figure, he felt, should be in the range of fifty dollars.

The day of the shopping trip I knew I was in trouble. I knew the other half of the team had something elegant and expensive in mind. Breaking the news to her wasn't going to be easy. I took what I thought at the time was the only sensible approach. We went out for a nice lunch at a rather expensive restaurant. We had a delightful meal with two glasses of dry white wine, and I avoided as the plague the question of the budget restriction.

Finally the meal was over, the table was cleared, and the subject could no longer be avoided. "What's our budget for the shopping trip?" my friend asked, and I knew that I couldn't put it off any longer.

Lowering my voice as much as I could, I braced myself and said, "The president has suggested that we limit our purchase to something under fifty dollars."

"*Fifty dollars?*" she shouted in a tone of outrage and horror. In an instant there wasn't a sound in that room, and I knew that I could have stood up and said, "Honestly, we were talking about Eskimo carvings," and not a soul in the room would have believed me.

You might think that the law would be relatively free of situations which lend themselves to a touch of humour, but consider the wire services item fed to every newsroom across the country, an item that originated in Denver, Colorado.

The Colorado Bureau of Investigation last week sent out a directive to all law enforcement agencies across the Rocky Mountain State which read as follows: "Fortunately, the message we asked you to disregard was not sent. Thus, we ask that you disregard the message we sent asking you to disregard the last message."

When a wire service item arrives at the desk in a newsroom, someone must decide whether to use it or not. If they decide to use it, a suitable headline must be composed. The job of the headline is to catch the eye of the readers, making them want to read the story printed beneath it.

They were certainly successful from that point of view on February 12, 1970, when the *Edmonton Journal* decided to run a story out of Vancouver. They headlined the piece "More babies a no-no for unwed father of 3."

The story originated in Vancouver, was attributed to the Canadian Press, and began:

Dale Martin, 22, an entertainer, Wednesday was ordered by a provincial court judge to avoid making anyone else pregnant for the next three years.

The order not to impregnate any girls came from Judge

Les Bewley, who gave Martin a suspended sentence and the three-year probation for possession of an offensive weapon.

"Does the order apply if Martin marries?" asked defence lawyer Jack Cram. "Yes," said the judge. "He will have to get written permission."

And so some cold winter's night, we may all draw comfort from the thought that somewhere in this great land of ours there may very well be a groom who turns to his bride and says, "It's all right, honey, I got a note from the judge."

I learned still another lesson about the business of being funny while doing items for the Edmonton CBC radio outlet. I had been supplying a daily humour piece to the station when the CBC network out of Toronto indicated an interest in using them on a syndication basis. The items I had been doing for the local station ran about three minutes, perhaps a little longer. The network items had to fit a regulated time slot. They had to be a maximum of two minutes and forty-five seconds in length, preferably even a touch shorter. That gave the network time for a brief introduction and then the item, both of which would fit into a three-minute hole.

I was rewriting the items I'd done locally, making sure they were tightened up to fit the shorter time period. It was after I'd been doing the editing for a few weeks that I realized that all of my tightening was taking place in the opening paragraphs. I was quite happy with the *body* of the items, I was just taking too long getting into them. I was getting ready to prepare to commence to begin to tell my story. I found that the only thing I had to change was the length of time it took me to get down to business.

With very few exceptions, you can find something humorous in any topic. The easiest ones to poke gentle fun at are the topics that, on the surface, seem the most serious. You can give religion a gentle nudge in the ribs without really hurting anyone. My mother and father were faithful members of First Presbyterian Church in downtown Edmonton all the years of their churchgoing lives. But the nature of the church changed over that period of time as the downtown core of the city changed. Instead of the somewhat traditional place of worship that First Presbyterian had been, it became somewhat of a drop-in church for people living in the centre of the city. It attracted people from a variety of walks of life and a variety of branches of the Christian faith.

My mother tells of the Sunday morning that the congregation was rather startled to find that someone had joined them who was apparently of a more vocally-demonstrative background. The man shouted at various intervals during the service, "Praise the Lord!" Now, while that's an accepted part of the worship service in many churches, it is not, I would gently suggest, a part of the worship service at First Presbyterian Church.

My mother says that an emergency meeting of the kirk session was held in the vestibule at the back of the church and the oldest and most dignified member of the session was delegated to go down and speak to this fellow before he disrupted the entire service. My mother says that the elder, in all his dignity, walked down the aisle, leaned over, and tapped the fellow on the shoulder, saying, "I'm sorry, sir, but we don't praise the Lord in this church."

The element of surprise is what you are looking for, the ending that catches and delights the listener, giving everyone's mind a rest before you push on with the heavier material at hand.

When you are preparing an address, you don't normally have a battery of funny stories you can tell about your topic. So when you want to brighten things in a funny way, or ease up with a relevant but humorous story, where do you turn? Is there a "joke book" recommended for this sort of thing?

The humour section of your local book store is usually stocked with a reasonable number of volumes filled with stories that are funny to someone. You may find that you are bored to tears with the things. The trick is to realize that you are going to have to do a little work on the material you find in any book.

A fellow called Robert Orben compiles short one-liners that can, if adapted, be used by many speakers. One of his books is called *The Ad-Libber's Handbook* (New York, Doubleday, 1969). Orben organizes his material by topic, arranged in alphabetical order. If you want to find a story that has to do with gardening, look under the letter G.

Let's suppose that you have been asked to speak to a local group about the changing standards in the world today. One of the points you might wish to make is that crime, particularly in urban areas, is on the increase. Turning to the letter c in Orben's book, we find a cluster of crime stories. As you read through the short pieces, you find one with which you feel comfortable. It brings a grin to your face as you finish it.

On page fifty-three of Orben's book you will find, "For the first time in history, even the churches are locked up. If you want to go in and pray, you have to go up to the door, knock three times, and say, 'Peter sent me.'"

As a rule, anything that *you* find interesting you can make interesting for someone else. If you find this little piece of business interesting, spend a few minutes thinking about how you might work it into your address, remembering that you want to make it relevant to the topic under discussion and that for maximum effect you want to sneak up on your audience and catch them by surprise.

You might suggest, in the course of your remarks about the changing times, that it's rather a sad note that even the churches in our urban centres are locked these days to prevent theft and vandalism. A terrible comment on what the world has become! If you want to visit a church during your lunch hour and have a quiet moment of thoughtful prayer, you can't get in. You have to step up to the church door and rap three times. A slot opens just about eye level, and you have to put your face up to the slot and whisper, "Peter sent me!"

And if you live in Alberta, there was a time when that covered you provincially, federally, and ecclesiastically.

The last sentence works with a western audience, but tailor the idea to suit *your* listeners. The tailoring doesn't take much time, and if you've done your homework effectively, your audience won't know you've snuck up on them with a brightener until you drop the "Peter sent me" shoe.

Bob Stanfield once called a press conference to complain about his treatment by the nation's media. When asked for an example of what he was worried about, Stanfield told the reporters, "If I mastered the art of walking on water, you'd headline the story 'Stanfield Can't Swim!'"

It's the twist that catches you and makes it work. It can usually be found tucked away somewhere, particularly when people are taking things a little too seriously. But remember that the operative word is *surprise*.

An extension of the "which reminds me of a story" taboo is that in humour you *show* them, you don't *tell* them. In an old *Mary Tyler Moore* television program, Rhoda Morgenstern was talking about a fellow she had dated. She could have said that he was cheap. Instead she said, "If he takes you out for dinner, you go to the kind of restaurant where you shout your order into a clown's mouth."

You could say that an Irishman had had perhaps a drop too much on St. Patrick's Day, but isn't it better to suggest that he's been downed by the old Bushmill's stream?

E. B. White had some interesting things to say about humour in the preface to *A Subtreasury Of American Humor* (New York, Coward-McCann, 1941).

There is often a rather fine line between laughing and crying, and if a humorous piece of writing brings a person to the point where his emotional responses are untrustworthy and seem likely to break over into the opposite realm, it is because humor, like poetry, has an extra content. It plays close to the big hot fire which is Truth, and sometimes the reader feels the heat.

The world likes humor, but it treats it patronizingly. It decorates its serious artists with laurel, and its wags with Brussels sprouts. It feels that if a thing is funny it can be presumed to be something less than great, because if it were truly great it would be wholly serious.

Later in the same piece, White quotes Mark Twain, who once said, "Humor must not professedly teach, and it must not professedly preach, but it must do both if it would live forever."

But White concludes his remarks by saying, "I don't think I agree that humor must preach in order to live; it need only speak the truth—and I notice that it usually does."

CHAPTER 7

The Language That the Stranger Doesn't Know

The sneakiest hurdle on the way to winning the public-speaking sweepstakes is sneaky because most people don't even realize that it is there.

No matter what you are discussing, from sewing to cybernetics, there is a special language that helps you to talk about your subject. The more you know about your topic and the more comfortable you become with the language of that topic, the less conscious you become of the jargon you are using.

If you don't know a thing about the game of curling, you will be baffled by references to in-turns, out-turns, drawing to the button, and coming out of the hack. The whole thing sounds mildly suggestive, but to a curler it all makes a great deal of sense.

When we are talking about something which to us is a very familiar topic, we tend to lapse into the jargon of that topic, forgetting that the *topic* may be of interest to our listeners but the jargon we use to explain it might just as well be Swahili.

Turn back to Funk and Wagnalls for a moment and you'll find that one of the definitions of jargon is "the technical or specialized vocabulary or phraseology used among themselves by members of a particular profession, sect, or similarly restricted group." If it's just "among themselves" there's no harm done. But when they try to include others in their conversation, the fun starts.

Recognizing jargon isn't the hard part. We recognize it all the time when *other people* are using it. The prime problem is realizing that *we* are using it. You always spot the jargon in another's conversation, but you must be constantly on the alert to catch it in your own.

A learned academic once sent to senior members of his staff a memorandum that read, "The working time frame of a staff member, interfaced with the curriculum load needs of the student body, is, in essence, an incremental non-formula approach based upon historical, current, relevant data, and government guidelines." He seemed surprised when people had some difficulty understanding what he was talking about.

It's a shame to pick on the academics in the crowd, but they do have a tendency to come up with good examples of the jargon problem. Ann Landers, that fountain of knowledge and advice on all things, on July 26, 1977, included in her column the following exchange:

Dear Ann Landers:

You are supposed to be a smart cookie. Can you figure this out? I bet my wife $10 you'd flunk just as we did.

The parent of a Houston high school pupil received a message from the school principal concerning a special meeting on a proposed new educational program.

The message read: "Our school's cross-graded, multi-ethnic, individualized learning program is designed to enhance the concept of an open-ended learning program with emphasis on a continuum of multi-ethnic, academically-enriched learning using the identified intellectually gifted child as the agent or director of his own learning. Major emphasis is on cross-graded, multi-ethnic learning with the main objective being to learn respect for the uniqueness of a person."

The parent responded: "Dear Principal: I have a college degree, speak two foreign languages and know four Indian dialects. I've attended a number of country fairs and three goat ropings but I haven't the faintest idea as to what the hell you are talking about."

OK, Ann, do YOU know what the principal was trying to say?

—Two Dummies in Fort Worth

Dear Friends: I don't think you are dummies. That principal needs to learn how to express himself in simple terms.

What he means is: "We are planning a program for students of all races which we hope will encourage the brighter ones to move ahead at their own speed. Grading will be geared to the learning level of the student. In this way we hope to teach and grade each student according to his ability to learn."

Probably the poor principal had no idea that he was using terms that were difficult for others to understand. He uses that kind of language every day, with his superiors, with his staff, in his reading, in all aspects of his working life. It was natural for him to use the familiar language when he *thought* he was passing the word along to others.

A newspaper reporter dug into the files of the Department of Education in Alberta. A survey of the reports circulated within the department showed a marked tendency to lapse into educational jargon. One of the examples the reporter presented in her story was, "The conceptualization reflected as a dominant characteristic of the information dissemination process of the provincial government department of education of a projected annual expenditure of half a million dollars does not fit within the parameters of comprehension exhibited by many educators who must digest the aforementioned information." Then she came up with the translation: "The provincial government spends close to $500,000 this year on educational reports that are often unreadable."

The whole jargon business poses a threat that goes far beyond the lectern of the public speaker. Our society has become so accustomed to the use of jargon that we tend to look at things that *don't* use jargon as being somehow suspect. We look upon things put simply as being less accurate or having less merit than those which are laced with the new language.

A manager circulated a memorandum to seventeen members of his staff. Without further editorial comment and without touching a word of the memo, the document that he distributed read like this:

Re: Input-Output

Careful analysis and review of division operations and programs reveal critical weaknesses in the area of input and output. For example, study of our operations shows we usually lack outside input, which results in a related failure of inside output. We also exhibit a very low level of inside input which also serves to limit our outside output. Therefore, we must immediately generate more inside input and outside input to create a situation where our inside output is greatly increased. However, as you know, inside input, outside input and inside output are closely linked to outside output which, in turn, is a function of total input-output. Therefore, in order to promote total input-output, we must upgrade our outside input, and inside input, as well as our outside output and inside output. That way we will be able to promote greatly increased input-output by virtue of our improved input-output, inside-input, inside-output, outside-output, input and output.

Please keep this in mind while preparing all reports.

The most frightening aspect of the whole story is that of the seventeen people who received copies of that memorandum, only three realized that it was a joke. As a matter of fact, some of the staff members took the memo so seriously that they wrote back. I would have given my eyeteeth to have had a look at some of the replies, but my management friend seemed to think that he had to draw the line of discretion somewhere, so he drew it right in front of his filing cabinet.

Everyone falls into the jargon trap. Have you ever had a conversation with someone who flies an airplane? They do it with letters. A pilot may look you right in the eye and say, "Did you know that MOT regs specify that when flying VFR through a CADIZ in CDA you should call your IFF to the nearest ARTCC?"

You would be perfectly justified in saying that you didn't know that, even if you were aware of the fact that what he really said was, "Ministry of Transport regulations specify that when you're flying under the Visual Flight Rules through a Canadian Air Defence Identification Zone, you should call your Identification Friend or Foe to the nearest Air Route Traffic Control Centre."

Canadian pilots carry with them a little grey book that's called the *VFR Supplement*, published by the Ministry of Transport and the Chief of the Defence Staff. I was curious about all the alphabetical abbreviations they use in their flying jargon. I turned to the front of the book, found the section on abbreviations, and learned that between the letters AAE (which means Above Aerodrome Elevation) and the letter Z (which means either Greenwich Mean Time or VHF Station Locator Marker) there are a total of 399 other abbreviations. How would you like to run that up your AVASIS and see if anyone salutes? (That's Abbreviated Visual Slope Approach Indicator System, in case you were concerned.)

When you are preparing a talk, you will probably find that some of the terms of your topic are going to form a necessary part of your material. That's fair enough. Your audience *should* be introduced to the language of your subject, but take the time to make sure they understand your terms. *The Canadian Press Style Book* ([The Canadian Press, 1974] 37) says that "with few exceptions abbreviations should not be used for first mention of an organization in a news story. Two things determine permissibility: frequency of use (that is, public familiarity in Canada) and context of the story. It is not possible to set lasting rules; what is familiar this year may not be a couple of years from now." *The Style Book* goes on to list a few of the more familiar and permissible abbreviations: AFL-CIO, BBC, CBC, CTV, CNR, CP RAIL, NDP, RAF, RCMP, UN, YMCA, YWCA, and MP.

Looking over your address with an eye for the jargon traps should help you to spot them without difficulty. Translating them so that your audience stays with you while you touch on them isn't too tricky either. The only danger is still the one that we first mentioned. We're all conscious of the other fellow's use of jargon but rarely conscious of our own. But if you are aware of the problem, you've got it more than half solved.

An excellent way to take the sting out of the jargon jungle we fight each day is to think how lucky we are that jargon didn't exist back in biblical times. How would the story of

Moses sound if, when he was leading the Children of Israel out of bondage in the land of Egypt, he'd had to work with our system? Perhaps something like this:

When they came to the edge of the Red Sea, Moses called a meeting and, with the agenda circulated in advance, opened with the reading of the minutes of the last meeting, at which time it had been moved, seconded, voted upon, and carried that they flee the land of Egypt.

There being no errors or omissions, Moses then said, "Since the only business arising out of the minutes would appear to be the crossing of the Red Sea, what sayest thou, Amminadad, to the problem close at hand?"

And Amminadad spake, saying, "I propose that we break off into study sessions to do an in-depth analysis of the problem, leading to rôle definitions for each and every one of us, which could take place concurrent with the drafting of definitions for the proposed data-base matrix upon which we can sort out class titles, working titles, classification, and position numbers for all our people with a view to determining key activity areas for skill-oriented individuals, always bearing in mind that we must strive to be conceptualizing contemporary social and organizational values with a predetermined intensification of our attempts to minimize activities at the same time as we maximize results, monitored, of course, to maximize feedback."

And Moses spake, saying, "The chair recognizeth Jemuel, and what sayest thou to this matter?"

And Jemuel spake, saying, "We aren't ever going to get across the Red Sea unless we intensify our comprehensive operationalization of the innovative mode relative to raft building with positive reinforcing focussing upon predetermined available resources."

To which Abiasaph spake, saying, "Mr. Chairman, I move we make a three-pronged attack on the problem, breaking off into study sessions under the chairmanship of Shadrach, Meshach, and Abed-nego, to analyze in depth the structuring of the success indicators which would then become the basis of mandating responsibilities on short-run definition methodology, following which we could reconvene as a committee as a whole and consider the white papers submitted by the three study sessions, and out of that evolve a working paper which would contain the key activity areas and structure goal definitions giving us an institutional thrust in a direction that might enable us to conceptualize the directions we might pursue in our attempts to find a success area which could then lead to a way across the Red Sea."

At which point Moses would have lifted up his eyes unto the hills, from whence came a whole bunch of angry Egyptians. And Moses would have said, "Listen, Kiddies and Pals. If we're going to survive we haven't got time for all that verbal alfalfa. You say you want to escape to the other side of the Red Sea? Well, listen. This is what we're going to do."

And how's that for a subjective evaluation of the rôle of the leader in the problem-solving matrix inherent in the solution of a problem, biblically-speaking-wise?

CHAPTER 8

Don't Pull Up All Your Roots

The Irish must have a terrible time on March 17 each year, what with all the people around them trying to affect an Irish accent. On January 25 the Scots don't seem to have quite the same problem as they work their way through the celebration of the birthday of Robert Burns. But the Faith and Begorrah Brigade are out in full force on St. Patrick's Day, whether they hail from County Cork, Ireland; Tickle Bay, Newfoundland; or Whiffin Spit, Vancouver Island. There's something about an affected accent that ranks right up there with fingernails on the blackboard.

Whether you are talking to a group of one or an audience of hundreds, there will come a time when the question of telling a story with an accent will come up, and the question won't go away until you have dealt with it. There are literally scores of wonderful, warm, delightful stories out there. Some of them deal with the Scots, some with the Irish, some with the Italians. If you worked at it, you could probably come up with a great yarn dealing with any ethnic group in the world. If all these warm wonderful stories are out there, why not use them?

Because the chances of backlash are just too great! We have to remember that when we affect the accent of an ethnic group, we are patronizing that group. We have wandered into treacherous territory and must be very careful where we place our feet. We have done terrible things to the story with an ethnic background, not just by the inept accent that we try, but by the cruel twist that has crept into so many of our ethnic jokes.

If you are down in Minnesota, you can pick up a little yellow-covered paperback book filled with Norwegian stories. In Chicago you can buy yourself a copy of a book filled with Polish jokes. But when you read these books you find a feeling of familiarity to many of the stories. In Eastern Canada they are called Newfie jokes, in Western Canada, Ukrainian jokes. It doesn't really matter what you call them; they are all the same kind of story. They tend to put people down, to hurl a little ridicule in their direction. If you turn to that kind of story, you never score enough points in the game of life to make it worthwhile, be it at a cocktail party, in a classroom, or during an after-dinner address.

The strange part of all this is that about halfway between the two extremes, the artificial accent and the cruel ethnic joke, there is a point where ethnicity and warm understanding meet, and the result is fertile ground for the public speaker.

Because of the inherent cruelty in ethnic jokes, most people tend to leave them strictly alone. When we do that, we walk away from a very rich heritage that is part of the Canadian national treasure. We are a country made up of many cultures. When we deny this aspect of our history, we leach a great deal of the colour out of our national fabric.

I worked for a number of years with a man who had grown up during the Depression on a farm near Sturgis, Saskatchewan. The community was about evenly split between Ukrainians and Scandinavians. Because my friend had a good ear for the spoken word, he could tell stories with either a Ukrainian or a Scandinavian accent. There was never anything cruel about his anecdotes, and they took on a richness because of the slight trace of accent that was thrown in free of charge.

One of the most poignant stories of the Depression years in the Canadian West is told by my friend. He is of Ukrainian descent and says that he was too young to be really aware of the Depression, but he remembers being a child on a Saskatchewan farm during that difficult period. He remembers that none of the farmers had enough equipment or money to operate a farm efficiently, and that they used to trade services amongst each other to keep things going. He says that for him, the Depression is summed up in a conversation he remembers overhearing, a conversation between his father and the fellow on the next farm, when his father said, "Hey, Wictor. You trash me, I gonna plow you back."

If we ever drop that kind of story because we've become overly cautious about hurting people, then we have indeed lost a very rich part of our historical and cultural past.

Peter Ustinov is a master of many accents, and to most ears he sounds authentic. We listened to Ustinov one night as he told a story that had him switch from a German accent to an Austrian accent. We could *hear* the difference, and we were delighted. We discovered that friends of ours from Vienna had seen the same program. Like Queen Victoria, they were not amused. When asked about the Ustinov *Austrian* accent, they said it was like someone from Dallas trying to sound like someone from Boston. No matter how close you come, there's always the chance that it won't be close enough for some of your listeners and they will, mentally, turn away from what you are saying because of it.

One morning I tackled a short piece for radio, a piece in which I talked about the young man two doors from us who had been given a drum set for Christmas. I talked about the way he beat upon his new drums morning, noon, and night, to the point where everyone in the neighbourhood spent their spare time straightening pictures on the walls. I said that we all suspected that he was talking to the Swahili in drum language. The piece was just nicely finished when the director signalled that there was a telephone call for me. When I answered, a charming lady asked if I was not aware that Swahili was a language and not a tribe, and that while the young man might have been talking *in* Swahili, he could not have been talking *to* the Swahili. I asked, as politely as I could, how she happened to know that, and she told me that she happened to have her doctorate in West African history. She was very nice about it, but she wanted me to get it *right*.

Getting it right covers not just the facts, but the accent as well. If you're *from* Boston and want to use a Boston accent, you're going to be just fine. If you're from New York's Lower East Side, you too have a wealth of material from which to draw and an accent to make it authentic. But if you're from

Boston and try to *sound* like someone from the Lower East Side...well, it's probably safe to say that never the twain shall meet.

Having said that, let's look at this from a different point of view. If there's a touch of something interesting in *your* ethnic background, why not make use of it? It can be one of the most effective weapons in your personal arsenal.

I was born in Canada but my mother and father weren't. They were born in Scotland. I grew up surrounded by people who talked with a Scottish accent, but I am extremely careful about the time and place where I will attempt the accent myself.

The interesting thing is that you don't have to meet the issue head on. There are turns of phrase that are particularly Scottish, and if you can work these in, it *sounds* as though you're talking with an accent. A Scot does interesting things with the word "though." It comes out "thoe." "Here it is" and "there it is" become "here it's" and "there it's."

An Englishman will say, "I was that tired..." and a Welshman will softly say, "Look you," or "Mark you."

Canadians too have their little tricks of speech. Where else in the world will you hear people say, "I'm not that fond of..." quite as often as Canadians do? Who else will refer to a student of piano or violin as we do? If the girl across the aisle from you in Social Studies were studying the piano, you would say, "She takes piano."

It's the colour that you can add to your talk that makes a trip into your own background so worthwhile. I like to tell the story of my father and the village blacksmith back in Scotland. My father's family came to Canada in 1911, and apart from a short leave from the army during World War I, Dad had not been back to Scotland until he retired in 1961. My mother and father went "home" for six months and settled into the hotel in the little town nearest the old family farm, and Dad started to pick up the threads of a life he had left half a century before.

He discovered to his delight that one of his old school chums was not only still alive but still practising as the blacksmith in the nearby village of Wiston. My mother says that it was a rather emotional day that they rented a car and driver and made their way the few miles to Wiston village that my father might talk with his old friend. When they arrived my mother hung back as Dad made his way across the cobbles of the smithy's yard. He walked up to the blacksmith and said, "You may not remember me, but you and I went to school together."

The smith put his hammer down on his anvil, wiped his hand on his leather apron before he extended it, and then said, "Aye, Sandy. Been away?"

Stories that come out of your personal past don't, as a rule, offend anyone. In the blacksmith story, Scots and non-Scots seem to find it a comfortable way to point up one facet of the Scots character. A little judicious dipping into your own past, your own experiences, and your own heritage can often help you make a point in your own unique way.

In a world filled with as much noise pollution as air pollution, we have all tended to build little protective walls around ourselves that we might have a little quiet space. When things in the outside world become too much for us, we retreat to our own inner garden and rest for a while. As we grow older we seem to retreat a little oftener and stay a little longer. You can probably sum it all up in the words of the popular song of a few years ago, "Ev'rybody's talkin' at me, I don't hear a word they're sayin', Only the echoes of my mind." (Fred Neil, Coconut Grove Music, 1970)

As he moved into his declining years, my father felt that the one great gap in my educational background was the fact that I'd never been to Scotland to touch the roots from whence I'd sprung. He set about correcting that grievous fault, and father and son, just the two of us, went "home" to fill in the gap as best we could in the time available.

After we had settled in, Dad found a couple of his boyhood companions. They were alive, reasonably well, and anxious to talk. We rented a car, and I drove these three old Scots around the countryside. We took in sheep sales, dog trials, and Highland games. For the most part, they just talked and I just listened.

All the years that my father had lived in Canada he had been a faithful subscriber to a newspaper called the *Hamilton Advisor*. He paid particular attention to the agricultural news, and he was better informed about the Scottish farming scene than many Scottish farmers.

It had been a long afternoon, and we had stopped, the four of us, at the Red Hart Inn for tea before we called it a day. In the quiet that came after the waitress had left with our order, my father said, "I see where the price of lambs is down a wee bit at the last sale at Castle Douglas."

To his left, his old friend Wullie Haddow said, "Aye, Sandy, I have the same problem. But with me it's lower down in the back."

And to *his* left, Gavin Coates shook his head without looking up and said, "You're both wrong. The whole family moved to Australia in 1934."

Don't hear a word you're sayin', only the echoes of my mind.

Is that an ethnic story? Probably not. It comes out of an ethnic background, though, and it helps to make a point.

The danger in our avoidance of ethnic stories lest we offend is that we walk away from a wealth of material which deserves to be remembered, to be recorded, to be *used* when we are talking to other people. If we turn our backs on our ethnic backgrounds, we are turning our backs on one of the richest treasures that our families can leave us.

CHAPTER 9

Could We Have a Little Respect?

A public speaker, whether the audience numbers one or a thousand, has never gone wrong showing respect for the intelligence of the listeners.

The instant you begin to talk down to your audience, whether as a conscious or subconscious thing on your part, they are going to sense it and they are going to resent it. They may not even realize what is happening, but there will be a feeling of resistance out there that a sensitive speaker can detect as surely as the beginnings of a thunderstorm.

The slip can be as simple as that problem we talked about earlier: saying "That reminds me of a funny story." In the minds of some of your listeners, the implication is that they are too thick-headed to know that you are about to tell them a funny story. They don't want to be *told* that it's a funny story. They want to figure it out for themselves.

Any school teacher will tell you that they *know* when the class is with them. The students are involved, they are paying attention, they want to participate in the teaching process. The teacher has challenged their minds, caught their imaginations, and is making them work. There's nothing the matter with making your audience do a little of the work. It keeps them busy, it keeps them alert and their minds off the streets, and when things are working well they enjoy being part of the process.

Let's go back again to some of the earliest routines of the stand-up comics such as Bob Newhart. One of the Newhart classics deals with the men and women who face death every day in the course of their employment, the nation's driving instructors. Newhart takes us on a trip with a "typical" driving instructor. We're sitting right there in the back seat listening to what he has to say. You never hear the voice of the lady student in the driver's seat. You learn what's happening through the voice and the reaction of the instructor.

As a listener to this Newhart monologue, you are working right along with him. He doesn't spell out every little detail of what's happening. You figure it out for yourself, and you love him for it. Newhart is making his audience work a little. It keeps them on their toes, it makes them participants in the proceedings, and they get more out of it.

The trick is to get your audience to try to anticipate what's going to happen next. If the word picture you have painted is vivid enough, they'll be able to imagine what's coming up next and if things are really working well, they'll be a split second ahead of you.

The examples we're using deal with humorous stories and making the audience a part of the process, not because the same principle can't be applied to serious topics, but because it's easier to illustrate the point with a Newhart monologue or a classic by Gerard Hoffnung.

An Englishman with the unlikely name of Gerard Hoffnung addressed the Oxford Union one evening, and his presentation has become part of humour history. It's a classic example of making the audience do the work, and the laughter, if you hear a recording of that address, proves that the results were there. Hoffnung takes his time with his delivery, paces the thing nicely, and by the time he's finished has the audience jumping through hoops.

Hoffnung's premise is that a bricklayer has been sent to repair a building and injures himself while tidying up. The worker writes a letter to the English equivalent of the Worker's Compensation Board, a letter which reads:

Respected Sirs:

When I got to the building, I found that the hurricane had knocked some bricks off the top. So I, therefore, rigged a pulley and beam to the top of the building and hoisted up a couple of barrels of bricks.

When I had fixed the building, there were a lot of bricks

left over. I hoisted the barrel back up again and secured the line at the bottom. Then I went up and filled the barrel with the extra bricks. Then I went to the bottom and cast off the line.

Unfortunately, the barrel of bricks was heavier than I was, and before I knew what was happening, the barrel started down, jerking me off the ground. I decided to hang on and halfway up, I met the barrel coming down, and received a severe blow on the shoulder. I then continued to the top, banging my head against the beam and getting my fingers jammed in the pulley. When the barrel hit the ground, it bursted its bottom, allowing the bricks to spill out.

I was now heavier than the barrel, so started down again at high speed. Halfway down, I met the barrel coming up and received severe injuries to my shins. When I hit the ground, I landed on the bricks, getting several painful cuts from the sharp edges.

At this point, I must have lost my presence of mind because I let go the line. The barrel then came down giving me another heavy blow on the head putting me in hospital. I respectfully request sick leave. (*Hoffnung at the Oxford Union* [Vancouver, Total Records, 1954] TRC 1045)

That's all there is to the letter, but read by Hoffnung with just the right pacing and pauses, it brings to mind one vivid mental picture after another, and the audience ends up being an essential player in the piece.

A speaker who has a sense of the awareness of his audience will know when they are with him and when he has to give them a second to catch up. If the speaker starts off showing respect for the audience, they will sense it and hang in there with him through the heavier portions of the address, providing he gives them a mental rest from time to time before he goes beyond the limits of their attention span.

It may be relatively easy to see how a skilled speaker such as Gerard Hoffnung can develop something such as his brick-layer piece and present it to an audience with great success. But what of the speaker who has to work with material that is perhaps less hilarious?

You can take topics that range from bookmarks to wall-to-wall carpeting to a ruler stuck in a desk drawer and, if you set the stage properly and make your audience work a little, you can keep them interested.

Stop and think about it for a minute and you will probably agree that the greatest threat to peace of mind, emotional stability, and normal blood pressure are those things which get stuck in a desk drawer.

Look at those handy little telephone index gadgets! You select the letter of the alphabet, push a button, and the thing pops open at the appropriate page. Surely one of the greatest boons to mankind since the invention of the roller towel until...you put the thing away in a drawer.

You can shut the machine, listen to it click, check it twice to make sure it's closed properly, and then put it away in a drawer. The instant you close the drawer, the thing flies open again and there is no way you are going to get that drawer open without the aid of a keyhole saw and a bent coat hanger.

You would think that a simple thing like a ruler would behave when placed in a drawer, but don't count on it. Put the ruler in the drawer, push the drawer gently closed, and the ruler turns into a demon. It flips itself at right angles to its original position, climbs up on a box of paper clips, and braces itself against the inside of the desk so that you can move the drawer about three-sixteenths of an inch before it jams. You can slam that drawer back and forth until you're blue in the face and that ruler won't move. A flashlight, the narrow edge of the bread knife, and a great deal of strong language may cause it to move, but don't count on *that* either.

And be sure to watch out for the stapler. Put a stapler in a desk drawer, and the thing takes on a life of its own. That stapler is going to spring open, wedge itself under the lip of the desk, and jam into position. Staplers are smart too. They let you open the drawer just enough to get your fingers inside, and then they staple the ball of your index finger to the bottom of the drawer.

Scissors will, without fail, stay right where you put them in the bottom of the drawer until the drawer is closed. Then they spring open, jam the points somewhere in the dark depths, and lock the drawer closed as surely as though it were the main gate of the Tower of London.

Telephone books, which in daylight are at least ten per cent shallower than the drawer in which they are placed, swell in the dark and jam the drawer shut for all time. Now that they have come out with separate books for the Yellow Pages, you can jam *two* drawers shut at the same time.

If you don't have a desk drawer that jams, surely you have a cutlery drawer in the kitchen that does the same thing. Many an evening has been spent in stunned silence simply because a husband tried to open a cutlery drawer when it was held closed by a pot metal garlic press and two spatulas. The silence is finally broken by the voice of a wife who says, "You didn't use that kind of language *before* we were married."

What you as the speaker are trying to do is to get your audience to picture that ruler in there, flipping itself around and sliding up over the paper clip box so that it's jammed firmly in place. Everyone has had something jam inside a drawer. You are sharing a common experience and you are including the audience in your story, helping them to laugh at something which didn't seem all that funny at the time. You are helping them to see an old familiar situation but from a slightly different angle.

What you can do with a ruler in a desk drawer you can do with something as simple as a bookmark because it is always amazing to find the things that people use to mark their place in a book when they are going to stop reading for a while.

You used to be able to take the bus from Edmonton to Vancouver for roughly what you pay for a nicely-illustrated hardcover book these days, so you would think that we would take a little time and care in the selection of what we use for a bookmark when we are reading the thing. But no, we tend to grab the first thing that comes to hand, stuff it between the pages, and slam the book shut. If you happened to be making a peanut butter sandwich at the time and went to answer the front door bell, you would be in some sort of trouble. You would probably use the knife to mark your place in the book, but better that than the sandwich itself.

We once lost a perfectly good ballpoint pen for weeks and then we found it when we were playing Scrabble. It had been dropped into the dictionary in the course of another Scrabble game six weeks earlier. Someone had been checking to see if there was a second "e" in unmistakable, had flipped over to look in on Genghis Kahn, and had left the pen back at unmistakable. We found it when we were checking to see if unalterable would fit all the way over to the triple word score.

Another friend once lost an important letter from her Aunt Sophie. Aunt Sophie had long since gone to the big quilting party in the sky when we found the missing letter. Our friend would have found it too if she had gone back and read the last half of *The Gulag Archipelago* before she passed it on to us.

Bookmarks are hard to find when you are answering the telephone. Rather than rip a leaf off the African violet, some people have been known to slam a book down on the kitchen counter. When they started to read again, they found their book had mayonnaise soaked through three pages in either direction of where they had left off. You are probably better off to rip a piece out of the magazine that came in the morning mail. That'll give you something else to be upset about when you try to finish the final segment of the series you started three months ago.

Everywhere you turn there are topics that, with proper treatment, make the audience a participant in their presentation. Keep the language simple, the images bright, and don't do all the work yourself. It keeps the audience awake if they feel they have a little work to do.

A friend of ours said, "My wife's been talking to herself lately, but she doesn't know it. She thinks I'm listening." This didn't indicate any stress or strain within their marriage; it just meant that they'd had wall-to-wall carpeting installed throughout the house and they hadn't adjusted to the new acoustics.

There was a day when oak floors were the thing to have in the home. Waxed to a fare-thee-well and with the odd scatter rug placed at strategic locations, they let a fellow come around the corner from the hall, step on a small carpet, and skateboard his way across the living room. But hardwood floors had one very obvious advantage that you don't think about until after the carpets are installed. You could hear people moving around the house and that helped bring a measure of order to a confused world.

Before carpets a fellow watching a sitcom on the television

set could hear his wife walking up the hall, and he would have time to pick up the current copy of *National Geographic* before she turned into the room. With rugs all over the place she's suddenly standing right at his elbow, a little like the Ghost of Christmas Past. Her husband would be hard pressed to claim that he was watching the sitcom for its redeeming social significance.

I have seen a husband standing beside the record player, carrying on a very serious conversation with a wife who had headed up the hall to make a lettuce and tomato sandwich five minutes earlier.

There are husbands who are looking for something in the kitchen cupboard and ask their wives for directions in a voice loud enough to be easily audible in Mazatlan. She happens to be two feet behind him and tells him in a hurt voice that he doesn't have to yell, she can hear him perfectly well when he talks without raising his voice.

There are husbands who have wandered through a newly carpeted home, calling for their wives in a plaintive voice not unlike the fellow who lurched through the swamp looking for Chloë.

There are wives who have husbands appear at their elbow much in the manner of Marley's ghost but without the sound of the rattling chains, which would have helped to give *some* sort of warning.

Pity the poor wife who was carrying a cup of hot coffee into the living room. She paused to look at the roses on the dining room table and her husband caught up to her. She thought he was out in the garage bundling newspapers for the salvage bin when a mysterious voice right behind her said, "Hi there."

Her husband has a couple of serious problems too. First of all, he has to get her voice down an octave and a half to where it was before he came into the room, and then he has to figure out how to get the coffee stains off the ceiling and the chandelier.

The problem of getting your audience involved in the delivery of your address is all part of the challenge, but it's an interesting challenge and it's a source of great delight when you can cause it to happen.

CHAPTER 10

Then There's the Lectern...and the Microphone

There aren't many tools in the speaker's trade, but the lectern is one of them. The dictionary would have you believe that a lectern is a stand having an inclined, shelf-like surface on which a speaker may place books or papers. If you talk to someone who has used one of these instruments of the devil, you may find that he describes it in somewhat different terms.

One style of lectern is what you might call the "portable" type. This is a wooden arrangement that you will often find placed upon the head table at a banquet. It isn't fastened to anything. Its weight alone holds it more or less in place. On the front of this style of lectern, the side facing the audience, you will find a metal plate bearing the name of the hotel in which you find yourself. This plate is so constructed that it gives a nice contrast between the letters placed upon it and the background, that they might show up clearly in black and white photographs and in television film footage. You may find that this is the only part of the lectern that works well when in use.

If you are standing behind the lectern, you will find the sloping surface referred to in the dictionary. Across the top of the lectern you will find that there is a *flat* surface, usually quite narrow. Fastened to this horizontal surface is a small light fixture intended to illuminate your notes. This light fixture never works but it gives you something to fiddle with while you are checking out the lectern.

The flat surface at the top of the lectern poses a problem. You will find that it's not quite wide enough to hold a glass of water. You will try to put one there anyway, and then it's only a matter of time before the glass slides toward you, dumping its contents all over the pages you have carefully placed on the sloping surface. The glass never falls in the direction of the audience, where the spilled contents would do no harm. This is a scientific principle which has never been adequately explained in any of the journals.

When you attempt to put the lectern to practical use, you find immediately that there is a problem with the *sloping* surface too. If you place your notes upon it, they slide to the bottom of the shelf. This puts them down around your belt buckle, a position which is most difficult when you try to glance casually down at your papers without losing eye contact with your audience.

Being calm and relaxed, you simply push your notes back up to the top of the sloping surface and carry on, but you find that when you pause to turn a page or lift your hand from the stack of sheets, they all slide back down to the bottom again.

At about this point you slam your fist down on the sliding papers in a vain attempt to stop them from cascading to the floor at your feet, only to find that the force of the blow dislodges the wristwatch that you hung from the light fixture that doesn't work. You had put your watch there when you took it off your wrist because you felt that it should be placed somewhere for easy reference when you wanted to see how much time had flown by.

If you have spilled your glass of drinking water down the sloping surface, you may find that the moisture helps to stick the pages to the lectern. On the other hand, you may find that when you want to turn the pages, you can't because they've become glued to the wooden surface. Hotel drinking water mixes with old varnish to produce a gelatinous sludge which hardens when exposed to air.

There is a wooden lip across the bottom of this sloping surface, a lip not quite high enough to hold anything except the drinking water that you spilled earlier.

Mention was made of the fact that this style of lectern just sits on the top of a table. The person who places it on top of the table, you may assume, is nine feet tall. He always places the lectern so far away from your edge of the table that you have to lean forward to touch it. If you try to pull the lectern gently towards you, you will find that the weight of the thing drags the tablecloth with it, along with the dishes in front of the head table guests sitting three seats on either side of where you are standing.

If you wear eyeglasses, and in particular bifocal eyeglasses, you quickly learn another great truth about lectern design. The sloping surface for your notes isn't in focus for *either* of the corrections in your lenses. It's too far away for your reading correction and too close for your distance correction. This leaves you with many pages of fuzzy notes sliding down a wooden surface and onto the floor at your feet.

Some lecterns are very fancy. They have an electric clock which is placed for easy viewing and a small red light which can be activated by the chairman for the evening. He is supposed to flash it when you are running out of time and he wants you to wrap it up.

Don't worry about either of these technical accoutrements. The clock hasn't worked since the Boer War and the red light bulb burned out during a Rotary luncheon in 1942.

Since you are the guest speaker, you might assume that the lectern is placed there for your use. This isn't exactly true. It's placed there for the use of all the speakers who have had a word or two to say prior to your appearance. There will be a chairman for the event, there will be a report from a committee or two, and there will be the chairman of the Entertainment Committee, who wants to draw everyone's attention to where the bar tickets are being sold and what time they are going to shut off the booze.

Each of these speakers has prepared a few notes which he brings with him to the lectern. Having said his little bit, he no longer needs these notes. Rather than take them back to his place at the table, it's much simpler to leave them at the lectern.

When you finally get up there, you will find a stack of waste paper three times higher than the lip at the bottom of the sloping surface. Why nobody else's notes slide to the floor is another great mystery. They stay there and *you* have to do something about them.

There is usually a space beneath the lectern, and if you are really composed and in command of the situation, you will gather up the stack of rubbish in front of you and slide it beneath the lectern, knocking over the glass of water that the chairman placed there half an hour before.

Another handy little gadget attached to most lecterns is a thing called a microphone. It is designed to aid you in the projection of your voice to the room at large. It never quite works out that way.

The first thing you will find on approaching the lectern is that the microphone is between you and where you want to look. You will also find that the last person to use the microphone was either two feet taller than you or three feet shorter. To correct this little problem all you have to do is grasp the microphone firmly in one hand and wrench it into the desired position. Microphones always come with a flexible neck that enables you to twist them around this way.

A microphone, when turned on, has a unique way of objecting to being twisted around in this fashion. It emits a loud and raunchy sound not unlike the rude noises made by the camels at the zoo.

All microphones have a small switch enabling the speaker to turn them off and on at will. There is an entire school of engineering given over to the design of on-off switches that are invisible to the person standing behind the lectern. Seven people may have used this microphone before you stood behind it and it worked perfectly for each of them. Walk up to it, clear your throat, and begin to speak, and you will find that the Ghost of Demosthenes stopped by while you were sorting your notes and switched the thing off.

Then you begin an interesting little game called Checking the Mike. Sound men will tell you that you should never blow into a microphone to see if it is turned on. There is an accumulation of moisture from your breath which does unkind things to the microphone. Sound men have a disgusting way of describing this process.

You should tap the microphone gently with the ball of your index finger. The loud thumping noise that is heard all over the room is an indication that the microphone is now working.

Most microphones are referred to as "directional" mikes.

That means that they only work well when you are talking right at them. Turn your head slightly to one side or the other, or lean back to look up at your audience, and your voice fades as the melting snow before an April breeze. Raise your voice and move back *toward* the microphone and the roar shatters wine glasses at the back of the room, causing a sleepy headwaiter to snap to attention shouting, "I'm sorry, sir, but you'll have to have a jacket and tie."

At this point the microphone, for no apparent reason, drops four inches. You grasp it by the flexible neck and jerk it back into position. It stays that way for ninety seconds and then drops again.

You twist it back into place, shove your notes to the top of the lectern's sloping surface, pick up the thread of your address, and at that point the recording secretary of the organization to which you are speaking stands up and tiptoes over to the front of the lectern. He doesn't want to distract you, you see. With the very best of intentions, he points his 35mm camera at you, waits until the little orange light comes on at the back of his flash attachment, and then he takes your picture.

Your whole world turns white. Everywhere you look, all you can see is one glaring white spot. When you look down at your notes on the lectern, all you can *still* see is the one bright spot.

Three sips of water later your vision returns, you find your place in your notes, and then the microphone falls again. In a valiant attempt to appear calm and collected through all this, you reach up with your right hand and rest it gently on the side of the lectern. You then learn another fundamental rule of lectern design. Thou shalt never make a lectern that sits flat on the table.

You have a rocking lectern on your hands, and if you have the type of stomach that gets a little queasy when you walk across a wet lawn, you are indeed in some distress. There will come a brief moment when your unbalanced mind thinks that the lectern is sitting still and it's the room that's rocking back and forth. Reason prevails, and you realize that that's not true at all. The room and the lectern are fine. It's you who's rocking back and forth.

Sometimes when they are setting up the sound system, they err in the placement of the speakers. They will put the speakers in such a position that what you say through the microphone is fed by the speakers back into the microphone which, in turn, feeds it back into the speakers. The phenomenon is called "feedback." The result is a piercing shriek from the speakers that increases in pitch and volume until your head and the room are about to explode. In season it will attract a moose from as far away as Flin Flon.

You then learn one of the fundamental rules of hotel management. If you have an audio technician who sets up the microphones and sound system for a banquet, you wait until the after-dinner address is underway and then you send your sound man on an errand to Zanzibar.

Eventually order is restored and you can carry on with that which you came to deliver.

If the Planning Committee doesn't like the idea of a "portable" lectern in the middle of the head table, they may arrange for a free-standing lectern to be placed off to one side. These lecterns have the same familiar sloping surface but stand on the floor and are supported by a single narrow column of wood. The base is usually too small for adequate support and the column is never fastened securely to the base. If you thought the portable lectern rocked back and forth, wait until you touch one of *these*. The microphone for this type of lectern is usually placed off to one side on a stand of its own, making it physically impossible to speak into it while standing behind the lectern and looking at your notes.

In setting one of these lecterns in place, the audio technician is very careful to fasten the microphone cable to the carpet with wide strips of masking tape, leaving one loop sticking up in the air so that you can get the toe of your shoe through it when you are walking to the lectern.

But when it's all over, you will realize that the tools of the trade ended up working for you, and working well...as long as you didn't let them intimidate you.

Meanwhile, back at the head table, you have been introduced. Move to your place behind the lectern and take the very few seconds you need to make yourself comfortable. The room is going to be settling down during this period anyway and no one will be aware that you haven't launched into your brilliant oratory.

Adjust the microphone so that you are happy with it. Clear away the flotsam and jetsam that's been gathering and place your notes there. Make sure you have a glass of water at hand, look up at your audience, and say hello.

Even the most directional of microphones is going to end up being your friend. The sound systems that you find in place these days work well, and if you talk into your microphone you will be heard throughout the hall without undue stress or strain on either your part or that of your audience. Stand, relaxed, behind the microphone. Keep your mouth fairly close to it and talk directly at it. When you glance to your right or left, and you will want to do that at intervals to maintain eye contact with everyone in the room, just *tilt* your head slightly at the same time. That way you will be talking *across* the front of the microphone as you look to the side. If you simply twist your head to the right or left, you will move off the microphone and your voice will fade. It's a rather simple, natural movement. Try it and you will find it quite comfortable.

If you have removed your watch the better to see it, you probably picked it up after it fell off the light on the lectern. Just where you put it is another question, but don't worry about it. It will show up about this stage of the game and you can slip it back on your wrist, which is where you usually look for it anyway. And when your notes slip down to the bottom of the lectern and you feel that you have to tuck your chin into your chest to see what's written down there, you will be amazed at how much of it comes naturally to mind anyway.

Whether you are working with typed notes, hand-written notes, or one- or two-word clues written on recipe cards, move them off to one side when you have finished with them. If you have a few quotations or some statistics that you want to include in your remarks and these are on separate sheets, make a separate pile of them just to the side of your notes. And when you have finished with *them*, turn them over or put them to one side. It's not exactly Tidy Time at kindergarten. It's just that you don't need any extraneous material cluttering up your work area.

Don't worry about making a neat stack of the notes that you don't need any more. You can retrieve them later from under the lectern, from the table top beside the lectern, or from the floor. They are like a runway to a pilot taking off in his airplane: they are no good to you when they are behind you.

You will find that you don't miss the little light at the top of the lectern. The room is always well lit anyway. The wobbly lectern hasn't really been a problem after all and the microphone worked so well that not once did anyone shout "Louder!" from the back of the room.

Before you know it, you are down to the bottom of the last page and a familiar voice is saying something about thank you very much. The voice is familiar because it's yours, and everything has gone very smoothly.

You may even want to give the lectern a friendly pat as you walk away. It's been a good place to be for the last few minutes and you might even look back at it with a measure of affection that you would have thought impossible just half an hour ago.

CHAPTER 11

Dealing With the Spooks and Goblins

It would be nice to commit a few words of wisdom to paper and ease the anxiety of a person who is going to speak in public and feels frightened.

It would be nice, but it would be impossible because it's not that simple. The spooks and goblins are there in one form or another for all of us. The best we can do is to hold each spook and each goblin up to the light and check it for cloudy spots. We may not make them go away, but we can get them into perspective and reduce the harmful effects.

Consider a certain three-day conference of medical specialists being held in the Rocky Mountains. These people had come from all over North America to discuss their areas of expertise and to explore those of others. They spent their working lives in intensive care units. They were called in when it appeared that the lights were about to be switched off for the last time, and while they performed a very necessary part in the practice of medicine, their success rate wasn't all that high.

The conference was wrapping up with a banquet and I was the after-dinner speaker. I was happy with the material I had prepared. It was light and I hoped humorous, but there were a few kernels of truth tucked in there under the candy flavouring. Our hosts had been most gracious, the hotel was comfortable, and we'd had two and a half days to relax in the midst of some of the world's most tranquil mountain scenery. The night of the banquet I was a mess.

The dinner itself had been built around a main course of Cornish game hen, beautifully prepared in the hotel's kitchens and served in a manner that graced the meal. I couldn't eat. If I put something in my mouth it seemed to swell as I chewed. I tried small bites in an attempt to get something down and that didn't work either. My distress must have been obvious to those around me because finally a physician from Ventura, California, raised the subject and I began to talk about my stage fright for perhaps the first time.

I don't remember a great deal about what he said. Others around our end of the table took up the topic and in the talking, I began to feel a little better. Not much better, but a little. Perhaps it was the realization that it was something that *could* be talked about that helped.

My friend from Ventura told me to close my eyes and remember what it felt like to have an audience listening to what I had to say, to imagine them laughing in response to a story and applauding at the end of it. I imagined all right. I imagined so hard my teeth hurt, but I really didn't feel all that much better when it came time for my contribution to the evening's happenings.

I stood up, I talked, I felt a little better and talked some more. And before long I could see the end and I felt even better. The audience laughed, responded, and reacted, and all went well.

After the dinner we sat back at the table and took up the conversation where we had left it before I had been introduced. I was infinitely more relaxed at this point, and perhaps as a result of that I am more aware of the direction of the conversation. But through it all one point stands out more vividly than anything else in the conversation.

My Ventura friend said that if I had worked myself into a state where I couldn't enjoy a dinner such as the one we had been served that night, then something was very wrong. He went on to sum it all up for me by saying that it was my mind that had got me into that emotional state, and it was only my mind that could get me out of it.

Standing before a group of people and saying a few words of your own choosing is really an exciting challenge. If we manage to make it an agonizing experience then we're doing something the wrong way. We draw small comfort from finding that our favourite movie star complains so bitterly of stage fright that he has to find a quiet corner and throw up before he goes on stage. He may tell us that he suffers from stage fright, but we don't really believe it. He performs all the time, we tell ourselves, so he *must* be used to it by now.

This raises one of the most common misconceptions about this interesting little malady. It doesn't necessarily go away with the passage of time. It may diminish, it may fade to the point of disappearing, but it never quite vanishes in most people.

There are even those who will tell you that if you ever reach the point where you are not nervous at all, then you had better quit because you have obviously become so used to it that you don't take it seriously enough anymore. To which you can always shout, "Ha! That'll be the day!"

The obvious question then is why we should pursue an activity that brings physical and emotional discomfort. One reason is that, to the best of my knowledge, nobody ever died of stage fright. It's annoying, it's inconvenient, it's embarrassing, it's even frightening, but it's not fatal. The challenge then is to get this funny feeling out into the open, into perspective, and then under control.

When you are plagued by stage fright, you become very much aware of the same problem in others. While I was watching the effects of stage fright on another person, an extremely valuable lesson was driven home to me one night in the course of a high school graduation ceremony. I was sitting at the head table next to the lectern and microphone because I was to bring a word or two to the graduands. The audience included students, escorts, teaching staff, and parents. The dining room was full. The total attendance was somewhere in excess of six hundred. There were others contributing to the program, one being a young lady from the graduating class who was to sing for us. She was to be accompanied by a pianist, and when the vocalist reached the lectern beside me, I realized that she had a case of stage fright that would have made anything I'd ever felt look like a mild case of the sniffles. Every muscle in her body was tense and as she placed her music on the lectern, her hand trembled visibly. I could see it, but I'm sure that the people in the audience couldn't. Soon her whole body was trembling.

Things were so bad that I actually looked behind her to see what she was going to hit on the way down when she fainted.

The pianist played the introductory notes, the young lady stood up to the microphone, and then her voice, rich, charming, and true, filled the room. She might have been trembling all over but her voice was as steady as a rock.

Despite the way she had been feeling when she stepped up to sing, she seemed unhappy with the microphone. She didn't like its position. At the end of the first passage in her music I watched as she did more to clear up my stage fright problems than anything I've seen before or since. She wanted to move the microphone so that it was more directly in front of her lips. She knew that if she wrenched it into position, it would send a horrible rasping sound throughout the room, breaking the spell that her voice had cast.

Without looking down, she reached out with one hand as she came to the end of the first verse. Just as she finished the last note, she unplugged the microphone, held the plug just inches away from its outlet, and with her other hand she grabbed the neck of the microphone and jerked it silently into position. She then plugged her microphone cord back into its outlet and hit the next note in her song.

I came away from that night knowing that if someone who was suffering that badly from stage fright could perform with that much poise under pressure, then there was not necessarily a direct connection between degree of stage fright and success of performance. And if it didn't have that much effect on performance, then stage fright was really an annoyance that could be dealt with separately.

Learning to deal with it separately, I received another great lesson from a dentist. He was working on a patient with a very active gag reflex. I heard the dentist's voice, firm but kind, saying, "Breathe through your nose. Breathe through your nose." In conversation with him later I said that I hadn't been able to help overhearing his comment to his patient, and that I hadn't realized that breathing through your nose would help minimize a gag reflex.

"It won't," said the dentist, "but it gives you something to occupy your mind when you *think* you might gag."

If that be true when you are having trouble in the dentist's chair, isn't it at least possible that the same thing might be true when you are expected to stand up and speak?

You will notice that we are not talking about stage fright *after* you stand up to speak. That problem seems to take care of itself in most people. The only tricky time comes while you are waiting to do your thing. In terms of speaking in public, it's quite true that the hard part is standing up. If we're onto something here, then what you want to do with that mind full of anxious thoughts is to crowd the anxious thoughts out with other, more pleasant, thoughts.

There are many physical things we can do to set our minds at ease, or at least *help* to set our minds at ease. We'll take the physical things one at a time in the next chapter. For now, let's look at a few things you can do with your mind that will help to while away the time as you sit there dying a thousand deaths.

Did you really catch the name of the people sitting at your side? What do they do for a living? Where were they born? Where do they like to go on their vacation? Have they ever been up in a hot air balloon?

You may not particularly care whether anyone in the whole world goes up in a hot air balloon, but you would be surprised at the number of people who take that sort of thing very seriously. You are not planning a hot-air-balloon holiday in Burgundy, either. You are just moving your mind out of its own troubled area and forcing it to become aware of things around you. Are there flowers on the table in front of you? What kind are they? What do they do with head table flowers after the head table goes home?

That topic may not rank up there with whether armed nuclear warheads should be dispersed across the country, but it is something that your mind can work with in its hour of need. You are trying to get your mind off its problem and onto something else...anything else.

I once shared a head table with Fred Davis of *Front Page Challenge* fame. We were at a conference on diabetes, and the delegates were very serious about their discussions. They needed to be. It is a serious subject. I noticed that the distinguished guest was in deep conversation with the guests on either side of him. He was very intent on what they were saying. It was later in the evening that I learned that butterflies are a problem, even unto Canadian radio and television stars, and this was *his* way of keeping his mind off the boogies and at the same time meeting some fascinating people and learning of their concerns.

You can't always count on the person sitting beside you to help when things aren't going well with your stomach and your tensions. She may insist on dwelling in great detail on the problems she had in the recovery room after she had her gallbladder removed. In a situation like that, you might be forgiven if you excused yourself from the conversation for a while and made a strategic mental retreat. People will understand if you tell them that you are going to look over your notes.

That's a little like telling your boss that you won't be in for work the next morning because you have to take a basal metabolism test. It may not be an authentic excuse, but it *sounds* authentic.

Get out a few sheets of paper, put them down in front of you, and withdraw int~ a quiet little world of your own. Like gardening? Why not give a little thought to a new approach to a flower bed you might get organized for next summer? Is sailing your thing? While doodling with a pencil, you may be able to draw a very rough sketch of the sailboat you would like to buy next season and you may find that your mind is out on the water for a few seconds, out where it's calm and pleasant and enjoyable. You don't have to stay there for long. A fraction of a minute helps. In fact, every little bit helps.

Do look at your notes. You've worked on them. You're happy with them. You're familiar with them. They are a touch of reality.

Tuck a colour print of a summer cottage or a mountain lake in among your notes. There was the night I took a small picture of a smiling granddaughter looking at me with the trust that comes from two-year-old eyes, and it was a great comfort to come across it during that tense period prior to the introduction.

The funny feeling may never completely vanish, but with a little luck and a little work you will push it into its proper place in your life.

In the winter you go cross-country skiing, knowing full well that in the morning you will ache all over your tired body. But that doesn't stop you from going cross-country skiing. You may be a long distance runner during the summer months, knowing perfectly well that while you are running your toenails are turning blue, your joints and bones are taking a pounding, and your muscles and tendons are busy preparing themselves to give you a bad time when the race is over. But you don't stop running.

During the warm summer months you may try water-skiing. As you sit there on the end of the dock watching the slack rope come up out of the water, not knowing that the seat of your bathing trunks is hooked over a rusty nail, you realize that there's a strong possibility that you are going to fall while travelling across the water at an unreasonable rate of speed. You are likely to pass three fish on the way down and swallow more water than you usually put in your bathtub, but you go water-skiing anyway and enjoy it.

Maybe stage fright is the sore muscle of the public speaker, but it isn't a good enough reason to pass up an opportunity that you will enjoy.

Stage fright exists. It is a very real thing and it can cause all kinds of physical distress. But I seriously doubt whether it ever stopped anyone from doing a good job once they got up on their feet.

When you are in the chair lift on your way to the top of the ski run, do you think about the sore muscles the next day or the thrill of the downhill run that's ahead of you?

Even when you think you have all the spooks and goblins under control, they may call on you in the wee small hours of the morning. They will gather around the foot of your bed and plant the thought in your mind that this is going to be the most embarrassing experience of your life. It won't be.

Things may go off track a little, true, but no matter what goes wrong, it won't be as bad as the night they put on the play in Vanderhoof.

I heard the story from a speaker at a technical conference in Calgary. He had graduated in engineering from the University of British Columbia and had ended up knowing a great deal about a very specialized topic. His field of expertise dealt with the cathodic protection of buried pipelines. He was invited regularly to bring his knowledge to various technical gatherings across the country.

The night I went to hear him his presentation, as usual, was built around a series of 35mm slides that he had taken himself. He was introduced at great length and with much fanfare, began his presentation, and then found that the bulb had burned out in his slide projector. He didn't have a spare. A runner was dispatched to pick up a new bulb and our friend moved to the front of the room and explained to the assembled guests that this was actually the *second* most embarrassing moment in his life.

When he had been an undergraduate, he explained, he had always been interested in amateur theatrics. He liked to perform before people, he said, and the "ham" in him really came out when he was at university. He had joined the amateur theatre at the University of British Columbia and at the end of each year, before the students headed out for their summer jobs, they put together a few one-act plays and took them on tour throughout British Columbia. After a couple of weeks of touring, they went about their individual summer business, then picked up the thread of university life in the fall.

They were playing Vanderhoof, a town between Prince George and Prince Rupert. Vanderhoof happens to be about the geographical centre of British Columbia, but that's neither here nor there. Vanderhoof was just a little logging community, he told us, but ready for this contribution to the local cultural climate that evening.

Just before the curtain went up on the first play, the stage manager came to our friend and explained that they were in real trouble. One of the female bit players had taken ill. It was nothing serious, but she wouldn't be able to perform that night. It was only a small part, but without it the whole play fell to pieces, and there was nobody else in the cast who could be spared to take her place.

Our friend and the stage manager headed up the main street of Vanderhoof and approached the first young lady they met. They explained the situation to her as quickly as they could and asked for her help. She said she wouldn't mind helping out, but that she'd never had any stage experience and wouldn't have any idea what to do. They explained to her that there were no lines to the part, she just had to step onto the stage at the right moment, and they would help her with her cue. The leading man would fire two shots at her from a revolver loaded with blanks, and then she would drop to the stage in the most natural-looking fall she could manage. They talked very quickly and very convincingly. She agreed, and with moments to spare they rushed her back to the theatre, slapped a little stage makeup into place, and arrived behind the set just as they heard her cue from the stage.

Our friend opened the door at the back of the set and the stage manager pushed the young lady out onto the stage. The leading man pointed his revolver at her and fired two blank shells. She dropped to the stage in a very realistic fall. The leading man dropped the revolver to the stage, buried his face in his hands, and moaned, "What have I done? What have I *done*?"

And a drunken logger at the back of the theatre stood up and shouted, "What have you done, you stupid twit? You've just shot the only hooker in Vanderhoof!"

That, said our friend, was the most embarrassing experience in his life. Think about it. If anything should go wrong on *your* big night, it won't be nearly as bad as that.

CHAPTER 12

Take the Time to be Really Ready

When the time comes for you to make your presentation, you have two primary objectives in mind: you want to do the very best you can, and you want to do it with a minimum of emotional upset and nervous distress on your part. There are a number of *little* things that you can do to help yourself achieve both objectives.

If you are bothered at all by stage fright, you certainly don't want to add to the tension by feeling any pressure from the clock on the wall. Before you leave home on the big day, have a clear idea of what time you would like to arrive at the appointed place, how long it will take you to get there, and where you will park when you get there. If your stomach has a tendency to turn into a hot hockey puck as the fatal hour approaches, you're only going to add to your distress if you get yourself stuck in a traffic jam somewhere or end up circling the block looking for a place to park. Build a little cushion of time into your plans for the day. It doesn't cost much and it can really pay dividends. If something does go wrong in the traffic department (and despite the best laid plans of mice and speaker, it can happen) keep a good thought. If it's an after-dinner address you are going to give, they really don't need you until they have finished dessert, and you don't normally eat salads anyway.

That line of thinking is small comfort, true, but it's best to prepare for all eventualities. With what you've got on your plate you don't need any surprises.

Arriving a little early for your engagement gives you a few extra minutes, minutes that you can put to excellent use by

attending to a few other little things that can make a difference. Prowl around and find the people who extended the
invitation in the first place. It helps, as mentioned earlier, if
you have a prearranged place to meet. The program people
may not really need you for an hour and a half, but they like
to know that you have arrived. If you think you are nervous
before you speak, just check the program chairman who
thinks his guest speaker hasn't arrived and the luncheon is
due to start in seven minutes. You may be a wreck, but he's a
mess.

That little extra bundle of time gives your hosts a chance to
meet you and introduce you to the person who, very shortly,
is going to introduce *you.* No matter what you have sent in
the way of biographical information, be prepared to find that
the person doing the introducing hasn't started on his introduction until the day of the meeting.

You'll be able to pick out your introducer in the crowd. He's
the one going through his jacket pockets looking for his
reading glasses, dropping the three sheets of biographical
notes that you mailed to him three weeks ago in the process,
and trying to write something down on the back of a paper
serviette with a ballpoint pen that seems to be out of ink. It
helps all around if you chat with the poor fellow for a minute.
It may not help him to relax, but it will do *you* the world of
good. It's always comforting to know that *somebody's*
emotional state is worse than yours.

You don't have to hang around the organizers at great
length. Having ascertained that you are there, they will stop
worrying. There are a few other things that need your attention.

Take a minute to walk around the room in which you are to
speak. See how they have it set up. Walk up to the head table
and see how much space there is between the back of the
chairs along the head table and the rear edge of the platform.
Hotel staff have an interesting habit of setting up a head table
on a raised platform that is just a little smaller than is needed.
They position this platform so that it isn't pushed up tight
against the rear wall. Often there's a reason for this. There
may be pictures, drapes, flags, or whatever hung along that
rear wall, and they don't want people brushing against them

as they walk in. They leave this space between the platform and the wall, a space that's usually about two feet deep and a foot and a half wide. It looks like the Grand Canyon when you come upon it suddenly, but it loses a lot of its power to startle if you are forewarned.

When all the chairs are pushed in close to the head table, there's lots of room to walk along behind them. When the head table guests are seated, on the other hand, you usually find that they have their chairs pushed back from the table. If you have to make your way behind the head table to reach the lectern, you may find that you are working with a path narrow enough to challenge a mountain goat. Since there's no other way to reach the lectern, you have to use it, but it's not easy. If you are a guest at a banquet and you see the guest speaker suddenly drop from sight on his way to the lectern, you'll know where he's gone. Give him a minute to climb back up, dust off his clothes, and compose himself, and he'll be ready to talk to you.

Head table platforms are always covered with carpeting. This muffles the sound of the people who have to move back and forth across the platform, and it gives it a more classy appearance than just bare boards. This carpeting is usually laid down in small sections. That means that there are joints in the carpeting, joints all over the place. Rather than leave any bare platform showing, the hotel crew overlap the carpeting, creating a series of ridges that are just about the right height to catch the heel of your shoe as you walk with great dignity to the lectern.

The wires to the lectern light and the microphone are always plugged into the wall behind the platform. To get from the wall behind the platform to the lectern they must cross the floor of the platform. These wires, along with the overlapping carpet, make for interesting footing. It helps a great deal to have had a look at it before your haunting hour arrives.

Have a good look at the lectern. Twist the little knob on the end of the lectern light and satisfy yourself that the light really doesn't work. Having that out of the road, you won't be tempted to fiddle with it when you stand up to talk.

Check the position of the lectern itself as it sits on the table.

Is it in a good position for *you*? If you want to shuffle it around a little, now is the time to do it, when nobody else is in the room. If you knock over the vase of flowers, there's time to clean up the mess.

Wiggle the microphone up and down to check it for height. You'll find out how stiff the flexible neck is and you'll often find that the instant you touch the microphone it comes loose in your hand. In the quiet of the empty room you can figure out how to put the microphone back on its stand without dropping it.

If you are planning to use any audio-visual aids, make doubly sure that they are all set up. If you are going to have an assistant run the projector, talk to him and make sure that the signals are clearly fixed in *both* your minds. Make sure there's a spare bulb handy, and that your handy-dandy helper knows how to change it in an emergency. Turn the projector on and make sure it's tilted at the right angle and that the screen you are expected to use is in a position where it can be seen by everyone in the room. You don't need the sound of two hundred chairs shifting into a different position when you are trying to make a serious point about the first slide that comes up on the screen.

A small point but an interesting one: if you want the room darkened for your slide presentation, find out how to darken the room. Hotels are built in such a way that it takes a four-year university course to find the light switches in the dining rooms. The poor fellow back at the slide projector is ready to go, you are ready to go, but nobody in the room knows how to turn the lights off. Find out where the switches are, have someone standing by to operate them, and have a prearranged signal so that the room doesn't go dark three minutes before you intend it to.

Another small but important point: turn the lights off and check your projector. You'd be surprised at the number of rooms that have the wall plugs connected to the light switches. There have been nights filled with horror when the speaker threw the cue to the light switch operator, who turned off the room lights and then headed for the chicken shack up the street for a burger and fries. Meanwhile, back in the dining room, the projectionist found that he didn't have any power at his projector. You now have a darkened room filled with confused people and a speaker wondering how he ever let himself get talked into a situation like that.

When things are running smoothly nobody notices, and when they aren't nobody forgets. Sort this kind of situation out in advance. It won't take a great deal of time but it can result in great peace of mind. It will remove some unwanted surprises and it will leave your thoughts clear for the prime task at hand, the successful delivery of your address.

During this period you may notice a certain dryness in your mouth. It's probably a direct result of nervous tension, and it's annoying more than anything else. At a time like this a few peppermint candies in a pocket may be the wisest investment you have ever made. A mint dropped onto the tongue keeps your mouth fresh, the saliva flowing, and your throat clear of cobwebs and other impedimenta that might remind you to tense up.

When the time finally arrives and you are ready to take your appointed place for the meal, you may have spent no more than five or ten minutes checking things over but it leaves you with the comfortable feeling that you are in charge of the little things instead of the little things being in charge of you.

Whether it's an evening affair or a luncheon, a meal will be served. You are expected to eat. Nowhere is it carved in stone that you *must* eat, it's just expected. And just as you are *expected* to eat, you in turn feel that you should.

If you're hungry, fine. Enjoy the meal and savour the sauces that they've poured over the chicken. If you're not hungry, then leave well enough alone. Forcing food on a stomach that would rather not have digestion thrust upon it is only going to create gastro-intestinal stress that you really don't need. The waitress serving you is not your mother. She will bring you your dessert even if you haven't finished your vegetables. The option is yours. If you feel that it's necessary, just tell the people on either side of you that you don't eat a great deal when you are going to speak and let it go at that. They will accept it and go on with their own meal.

If you do eat, eat carefully. If you are wearing a white shirt and you are about to stand up in front of all these people, be very careful of things that go drip in the night. You would be amazed at how often a forkful of spaghetti sauce will miss your necktie and dribble down the front of your shirt.

When a shirt is mentioned in this context, you will realize that the word shirt is interchangeable with the word blouse. The comments that reflect male wearing apparel are inserted purely on the basis of familiarity and ease. I've spilled gravy down a white shirt and smeared it when I tried to hide it with my tie, but I have also seen a female speaker drip a little Baked Alaska and chocolate sauce down the front of an imported French silk scarf just before she was to say a few words. She didn't feel any better about her scarf than I did about my gravy-stained shirt.

Just as it is not carved in stone that you have to eat everything placed before you, neither is it carved in stone that you must stay riveted to your chair throughout the entire meal. People all around you are intent upon their own food and the conversation across *their* table. Once the formalities of the proceedings have been dealt with (grace, head table introductions, toast to the Queen, or whatever) the room usually regroups into small conversational circles and head table people can move around without attracting undue attention.

If you feel the need, by all means excuse yourself and make a discreet trip up the hall. You might mention to your chairman that you'll just be a few minutes and that you're not catching a flight to Guadalajara. Make your trip and stroll up and down the foyer for a minute. Clear your head and throat. They're not going to start in there without you, and when you return you'll be pleased to find that nobody noticed that you were away.

Since everyone's throat behaves in a different way, it's a little hard to set out firm rules about what to eat and what not to eat if you are going to speak. As a general rule, gooey desserts are dynamite. They build a nice sticky layer at the back of your throat that no amount of rasping or clearing is going to cure. Gallons of water will not wash it away and you may find that the tickle lingers long enough to be a nuisance. I have known radio announcers who wouldn't touch a glass of milk with a ten foot pole if they were to go on the air. A few swore by a glass of hot lemon tea when it came to clearing the throat.

There are times when a small dab of whipped cream will create a tickle that a bomb wouldn't clear and there are other times when you can sit there and scoff three crème de menthe parfaits in a row and they won't bother you a bit. It's probably all in your mind and not your throat. But if you are looking for something to keep your mind *occupied*, fussing over the sugar content in the dessert is as good a thing to be doing as anything else.

I'm not sure if there's an exact feminine equivalent of this, but for a man, it's a good idea to empty your pockets before you stand up. This not only gives you something else to do while they're clearing away the desserts and pouring the coffee, but it also helps you to feel better when you stand up. A small metal ring with sixteen keys on it, two dollars in small change, and a pocket knife can make an incredible amount of noise if you put your hand in your pocket and jiggle it nervously as you speak.

You may very well have to blow your nose while you are standing there, but you'll only need one tissue to do it, not a wad big enough to plug a leak in an earth-filled dam.

Check your jacket pockets too. That billfold is loaded with credit cards, the flimsy copies of your last sixteen gasoline credit card purchases, two pink slips from the dry cleaners, and your lucky Bahamian three-dollar bill. All of this is nice to have close at hand, but the billfold doesn't do all that much to help your jacket hang properly. Take the thing out of your pocket and leave it beside your coffee cup. It will be right there when you come back and your suit will look the better for it.

Pens and pencils do interesting things to the drape of a jacket as well. You are not going to have to write anything down while you're at the lectern, so put them beside your billfold.

You are just about ready to go to work, and the fellow who is to introduce you is moving up to the lectern. It may prove tricky because you have a great deal going on in your mind at the moment, but *listen to what he has to say*, and make sure you've got his name straight.

When they finally do turn the microphone over to you, it helps all around if you can say something along the lines of, "Thank you very much, Murray, for that very generous introduction. Murray mentioned our three daughters and I would like to state, here and now, that there is no truth to the rumour that when our last daughter was married I wanted to have the congregation sing Hymn 468 in the United Church *Hymn Book*. Actually, I only *suggested* that we sing that hymn, but my wife vetoed it when she found out that Hymn 468 is 'The Strife Is O'er, The Battle Done.' "

Something like that lets everyone know that you were really listening and your use of the fellow's name personalizes it. The chances are that everyone else in the room knows him too, so now you're all friends. If you called him Murray and his name was Herbie then you are not off to the greatest start in the world.

All of this also gives you something to say while the room settles down. You can make a final adjustment to the microphone and get your notes out of your pocket and in place on the sloping shelf of the lectern.

Another thing that you might consider taking to the lectern with you is your own glass of water. The chances are that your throat is going to get a little dry. Whether it does or not, it's nice to know that you have a glass of water handy in case you need it. There's nothing quite like the knowledge that you *don't* have a drink of water at hand to make you need one.

They are usually very careful about placing a pitcher of water and extra glasses at the head table just so people can pour themselves a drink if they wish. If that be true, why then go to all the trouble of carrying your own glass around with you?

Quite apart from the fact that it gives you something else with which to occupy your mind, when you carry your own glass you *know* what you're getting. The hotel staff who are charged with setting out the tray with the water pitcher and extra glasses do it while they're setting the tables. That's usually two hours before you decide you want a drink. When you are thirsty, your throat is dry, and your lips are cracking, you might reach down and pick up one of these glasses that's been sitting there during the dinner. Just as you are about to soothe your parched lips, you notice that the glass of water has a layer of dust and a big piece of cigar ash floating on the surface. All of a sudden the idea of bringing your own glass of water with you doesn't seem quite so silly.

You are now standing at the lectern, you've said your first few words, and the room has settled down. Draw a measure of comfort from the knowledge that in three minutes you are going to feel much better than you do now, in *five* minutes you are going to feel even better, and in twenty minutes it will all be over and you will feel fine.

And we can all stand just about anything for three minutes, now can't we?

CHAPTER 13

The Demon Rum

Use a little wine for thy stomach's sake and thine often infirmities, as Saint Paul advised Timothy, but do it carefully if you have to say a few words later on in the evening.

This is a thousand miles removed from anything resembling a temperance lecture. It's more in the nature of a cautionary word, and that's all. Spirits taken internally tend to move directly to the tip of the tongue and you don't want your tongue to tango, particularly if you had a waltz in mind. You're not going to stand up there and do "Peter Piper picked a peck of pickled peppers" sixteen times as fast as you can. Neither do you want to get into trouble saying something like "shoe salesman" in the course of your remarks.

There is every possibility that there will be a social hour prior to the banquet or luncheon you are attending. There is an even stronger possibility that there will be wine served with the meal. If you are to say a few words at this luncheon or banquet, it's desirable that you relax and enjoy the experience as much as possible. Having a drink before the meal gets under way, and perhaps a glass of wine with your meal, could be a very pleasant part of the whole experience, but you are not exactly in the same situation as everyone else in the room.

Because you are anticipating the rôle you will be expected to play in the proceedings, you have something coursing through your system that makes you a bit unique among the assembled guests. To keep things simple let's just call it adrenalin. A little wine and a little adrenalin when mixed together can produce interesting results and unless you know exactly what those results are going to be, treading lightly is the best approach.

I was asked to give an after-dinner address to a meeting of the Scandinavian Society. It was a rather formal occasion, men only, held in a very comfortable private club in the heart of the city.

I believe that the Scandinavian countries are held to include Sweden, Norway, and Denmark, plus Finland, Iceland, and the Faroe Islands in some circles. The program for the evening was fairly well established by tradition. The head table was graced with a very nice array of the flags of the countries represented, and part of the evening's ritual was a salute to each of these flags and the country the flag represented. The salute consisted of the singing of the national anthem of the country, followed by a toast. The toast consisted of a glass of Aquavit followed with a beer chaser. The Aquavit was served by waitresses who held each bottle wrapped in a thick towel because it had been stored in a freezer so that it would be consumed ice cold. Aquavit, in case you haven't run across it, packs slightly more wallop than a mean mule.

As the toasts moved from country to country, a noticeable air of relaxation swept across the room. The chairman for the evening leaned over and very quietly pointed out that it wasn't really necessary for the guest speaker to toast each country with Aquavit and beer. A simple sip would suffice, and even the raising of the glass would be quite acceptable. They had had after-dinner speakers, he confided, who couldn't stand up after dinner.

The experience was vaguely reminiscent of that old radio comedian who used to talk about Uncle Slug, his drinking uncle. He claimed that Uncle Slug used to have the odd drink to steady himself, and sometimes he got so steady he couldn't move.

As the speaker, part of your problem is that you are so emotionally keyed up that you may not notice the fact that things are sneaking up on you until you try to stand up and say something. When you discover that someone has stolen all your bones, it's a mite late in the day to cool it.

During the dinner, if it's an evening affair, the head table is

117

usually well looked after. They had better be! They are the ones who are going to settle with the hotel when the affair is over. Waiters or waitresses will hover behind the head table diners making sure that their needs are met. While they hover, they will often top up your wine glass.

If you've been sitting there for an hour or so working your way through the dinner, then the business that had to be dealt with after the dinner, then the preliminaries to your talk, you may think that you've never quite reached the bottom of your wine glass. That is very likely true, but you've probably scoffed the top half seven times.

Just as you are not compelled to eat everything on your dinner plate, neither are you going to break anyone's heart if you decline the wine. If you'd like to shut the tap off completely, just quietly turn your wine glass upside down and place it back on the table cloth. Your waiter will get the message and he will not push, neither will he plead. It's your prerogative. Use it.

If you had a very important golf game to play, you would be very conscious of the need to keep your head as clear as possible before you hit off on the first hole. If you had a very important business meeting to attend during the afternoon, you would play it safe during your lunch. If you have an address to give after you've finished your prime rib and baked potato, treat that address with the same respect you would show for a golf game or a business meeting. I guess it would be called showing respect for the job at hand.

Once you are up on your feet and talking, there are a number of things that have to be fed into that computer you carry between your ears. You have to consider the passage of time, and you have to refer to your notes and lift the material that's down there off the paper and out to the audience through a microphone. You have to be alert enough to pick up changes that might be made in the course of your remarks, perhaps a point that needs expanding as a result of something you were told during the meal. All of these are little things and don't present a problem — as long as your mental windshield isn't all fogged up.

In short, the more alert you are, the better your chances of doing a good job. You owe it to your audience to do the very best job you can with the task at hand. What's even more important, you owe it to *yourself* to do the very best job you can.

Sometimes an external influence can keep you in touch with reality. I have a wife who will, on occasion, very quietly say, "Tell them the one about the three Indians." What she has in mind is a priceless piece of Alberta folklore. It tells the story of the three young braves who belonged to a tribe in southern Alberta living on the eastern slopes of the Rocky Mountains. The tribe had many traditions, one of which had to do with the firstborn child of any couple. Before the first-born child arrived in the world, the father had to go into the forest with his bow and arrow and shoot something which could be skinned. His wife was then charged with making a gift for their expected child using the hide of the animal her husband had slain.

Three young men of the tribe married three young women of the tribe one summer and in due course it was discovered, to everyone's delight, that each of the three couples was expecting a child. True to the tradition of the tribe, each young father headed out with his bow and arrows to kill an animal that could be skinned, that he might bring the hide home with him so that his wife could make a gift for their new baby when it arrived.

The first young brave headed north and after much hunting, he found a deer that was magnificent enough in shape and stature to be suitable for the gift for his baby. With his trusty bow and arrow he slew the deer, skinned it, and took the hide home to his wife.

The second young brave headed west, and after a long period in the forest came upon a mighty elk. He killed the animal with his bow and arrow, skinned his prize, and took the hide back to the village so that his wife might make something for their baby when it arrived.

The third young brave headed south and hunted for many days before he found anything. When he was about to give up the hunt, he came upon a hippopotamus. It took many arrows from his trusty bow, but he finally killed the beast. With great difficulty he managed to skin it, but skin it he did, and he headed home with the hide to present it to his wife.

In due time, the wife of the young brave who had killed the deer was delivered of her child, a son, and the couple were well pleased. Shortly after that, the wife of the young brave who had killed the elk was delivered of her child, and it too was a fine son. More time passed and the third mother, the wife of the Indian who had killed the hippopotamus, was delivered, and to nobody's surprise she had *twin* sons.

Twin sons, of course, because the squaw of the hippopotamus is always equal to the sons of the squaws of the other two hides.

Try that story after you've had three martinis and you will have even old Pythagoras holding his breath until you're finished. An added advantage is that even if you pass the test, it takes so long to tell the story that by the time you have finished, the bar is closed anyway.

CHAPTER 14

Radio is Still Around

The chance to say a word or two in public certainly isn't limited to the lectern, the classroom, or the sales meeting. Consider radio.

The wonderful world of radio slipped into the doldrums for a few years after television sets hit the market, but it has bounced back in a way that's affecting us all. Radio, at one time, meant the *Lux Radio Theatre* on Monday night, *Fibber McGee and Molly* on Tuesday, and *Fred Allen* on Sunday after the dishes had been cleared away. Today the content of radio programming has changed and the availability of a radio signal has changed. The family doesn't sit around the mahogany case of the Marconi that's parked in the corner of the living room. They take radio with them wherever they go, in the car, on a bicycle, to the park, even when they are out jogging.

True, music still plays a big part in any station's programming, but radio has reached out a little. Radio doesn't automatically mean background music these days. You get that in elevators and dentists' waiting rooms. If you want music to peel potatoes by, you can certainly find it on the radio dial, and in a style to suit your personal taste, but more and more, radio means interviews, public affairs programs, phone-ins, and just more general involvement with the community. Radio programming is no longer the syrupy voice saying, "That last selection was by the talented George Gershwin. And before that you heard...and before that you heard...."

The Canadian Radio and Television Commission has had a

hand in the change in programming as well. They have a little something they call Canadian content, and they have set standards for the amount of Canadian content that must be met by the stations. For whatever reasons, the chances of your being asked to say a few words on radio are infinitely higher than they were a few years ago, and it's an experience you might enjoy.

You may feel strongly about the city's plan to build a six-lane freeway through your backyard and a newsperson will stop by and ask you why you're upset.

You may have won the prize for the best-landscaped yard and garden in the competition sponsored by your local horti-cultural society, and your favourite radio station would like to send someone around to talk to you about it.

You may have been recognized by the chairman at last night's Home and School meeting, at which point you stood up and ripped off some cogent thoughts on the wisdom of offering rocketry classes to Grade Two students during their cookie break. Your points were so well made that the news director at the radio station wants to send a reporter around to talk to you about the problem.

There was a day when being asked to say a few words on radio meant getting yourself to the studios of the radio station. Once you had found the place, you sat down across a table from an announcer whose voice sounded like the big bell at Notre Dame Cathedral. You answered the questions that he read from a prepared script, and that was it. That may still happen, but it's more likely that the interview will be conducted in the comfort of your own living room, out in your front yard, or underneath the grease rack at the neigh-bourhood service station. It may even be held in the hallway outside the school gym where you sounded off about the rocketry classes, if the reporter was at the meeting and realizes that what you had to say might make interesting listening.

All of this flexibility has come about through the techno-logical changes that have been brought to radio broad-casting. A high-quality tape-recorder is so compact these days that it will fit into a purse or a jacket pocket. Some of the larger ones are a bit bigger than a shoe box, but the radio news reporter certainly doesn't have to lug around a truck-load of equipment to do an interview away from the station. The station now comes to you, you don't necessarily have to go to the station.

The change in the technology of the radio business has helped to bring about a change in the *sound* of the radio business. There was a time when the announcer bringing you the six o'clock news sat down with a carefully-typed script and read the story that was being presented to the listeners. Not now. The announcer may introduce the story, but then he says, "And now, here's Joe Finsterwald with the details." At this point the voice of the reporter takes over and he in turn involves the actual voices of the people concerned with the event. You've got variety, credibility, reality, and a lot of other things mixed into the story, and it makes for better listening. We are aware of this sort of thing in a news broadcast, of course, but listen to the other programs on the air these days and you will realize that they are doing the same thing with weather reports, sports, public affairs, and even the sale of merchandise. There's a great trend toward "remote" broadcasts during which a staff announcer is set up in a shopping mall, a furniture store, or an automobile sales room. When it comes time for the commercial message, it's out to Friendly Fred at the supermarket where old Fred has lined up a couple of sales clerks, the produce manager, and three customers to explain to the folks that they should really stop by and take advantage of all these bargains.

All of this means that your chances of being asked to say a few words into a microphone are a lot greater than they used to be and there are a few things about this aspect of public speaking that deserve consideration.

If someone asks you to discuss the topic in question or comment on a situation, they should tell you who they are, what station they represent, and what they would like to discuss with you. If they don't tell you, ask them.

If you choose to keep your thoughts to yourself, that's your privilege. It is not carved in stone that you *have* to think up something to say just because there is a microphone thrust in front of your face and a reporter is waiting for you to answer. You are perfectly at liberty to decline to comment. In most instances, your wishes will be respected and you won't be pressured. There is, however, a school of journalistic thought that sees nothing wrong with a question such as, "Apart from that, Mrs. Lincoln, how did you enjoy the play?"

If you run up against that kind of pressure approach, don't lose your temper. They may try to make you feel guilty. They may ask you if there's anything you don't want the radio audience to know about, the suggestion being that you are trying to hide something. They have a number of interesting ways to rouse your ire, all of which are effective only if they make you so upset that you forget that you really chose to keep your thoughts to yourself.

If you *do* choose to answer the question or agree to an interview, keep in mind that the tape will probably be edited. That's a term that really means that someone back at the station will chop out the dull parts and keep the good parts. This isn't, of itself, a bad thing. Very few people are capable of making their point briefly and effectively unless they give their answer a great deal of thought and write it down in advance. Editing is usually a tidying-up process that's necessary if you are going to hold the interest of the listener. Some politicians have become very adept at dropping a few zingers into an interview, quotations that they know can be lifted out of a longer interview and fitted into the six o'clock news. They can carry these little gems in the back of their minds and trot them out on demand. They make great listening and create the image of a clever mind and a command of the language.

You'll often hear people say that when they heard the interview on the air, they found that their remarks had been taken out of context. What may have happened is that, for some reason or another, a particular point was made but the qualifying remarks explaining why they held that view were trimmed off.

On the question of family planning, you might make the comment that, "Every young couple should have children, provided they feel that they have a stable marriage and that the prospects of bringing a healthy baby into a turbulent world fit into their long-range plans for individual careers and, of course, assuming that they both want to have children." You might find, when the interview is aired, that you hear, "Every young couple should have children." That isn't exactly what you had in mind, but that's what you hear yourself saying.

A good editor can do amazing things with an interview. With a little care on the part of the editor, the listener can't tell where the edits have been made. This can result in good things happening as well as bad. You can make a lengthy statement defending motherhood and the flag and end up sounding like Attila the Hun on a bad morning. But you can also stumble your way through an interview and, with a little help from the editor, end up sounding like Albert Schweitzer.

A former CBC Public Affairs man came back to the station carrying a long taped interview with a stroke victim. The man's speech had been impaired to the point where he had extreme difficulty in putting his thoughts into words. He had been working with a therapist, and he was making progress, and he wanted to tell other stroke victims that they shouldn't give up. It was an agonizing thing to hear, but with skillful editing the finished interview retained the intensity of the man's feelings along with his essential point of view, and good things happened when people heard it broadcast.

Remember too that a tape recorder can be stopped. It can be reversed so that the tape backs up. If you've lost your train of thought, *tell* the reporter and ask him to roll the tape back so you can start again. He may act as though he's performing the lead rôle in *Camille*, but that's all right. It's not he who's going to sound inept if they run the original taped answer on the air.

Even in the comfort of your own home or front yard, you may feel a little strange as you stand there answering questions. A good interviewer will chat with you for a while, helping you to relax in this strange situation. He should explain what's going on, show you how he will hold the microphone, and in general try to put you at your ease. All of this is nice, but it may not help all that much. When you are standing there having questions fired in your direction, psychology is working against you.

You are going to feel very self-conscious. You are in a strange new activity and you aren't sure how it will work out.

You would like to do well, but away back in a dark corner of your mind is the fear that you will sound like an idiot before the whole world.

The reporter is ready to go, and he holds the microphone to his lips, looks into your eyes, and asks you a question. The instant you start your answer, he shoves the microphone in front of *your* lips and then looks down at his tape machine. You might think that he's not listening to your answer, but he really is. He's probably just checking his tape recorder to make sure that it's running properly, and he's looking at the little meter that shows him the level of your voice as it goes down on the tape. For you, it's still very disconcerting, but only if you don't know what's happening.

In the meantime, you stand there trying to make your statement briefly, simply, and intelligently. It's not easy because one of your kids just came out the front door with peanut butter all over his face and he's headed your way, the mailman is walking up the other side of the street and looking back at you over his shoulder, and your neighbours who just drove past almost rear-ended a dry cleaner's van as they tried to see what you were doing. You haven't felt this self-conscious since the day you got a speeding ticket and everybody in town drove by while the policeman was writing it up.

If the interview is moving along nicely and a question arises that you're a little uncertain about, why not ask the reporter if he'd mind repeating the question? He will, and the implication is that his question had been badly phrased the first time he asked it. He will rephrase the question, using three times the number of words he did originally. Since you heard him the first time, you can gather your thoughts together while he's running it past you again. You can make psychology work for you too, you know.

It's extremely difficult to remember at the time of the interview, but if you are aware of any speech habits you have that can be eliminated, try to trim them off before they go down on tape. If you have a tendency to start each sentence with "well" or "now" or "like," you will be very conscious of those vocal clichés when you hear your interview played back. Trying to launder your language during the course of the interview may make you so self-conscious that you end up knocking out all the "likes" but failing to make your point. A comfortable linguistic style comes with practice; it cannot be suddenly acquired during the course of an interview.

If you are approached about an interview, your instinctive reaction is to ask the reporter when he would like to conduct it. You feel flattered, and it shows. That's very thoughtful of you, thinking of *his* needs, but you should be thinking about *your* needs. When would it be convenient for *you* to be interviewed, and where would *you* be most comfortable? Interviewees have rights too!

Portability of equipment notwithstanding, that invitation to say a few words for the vast listening audience may take the form of a request to visit the radio station and have the interview conducted there. If this should be the case, the interview will either be taped for release at a time more convenient for you and the station or it may be a live "on air" situation. Whether your interview is going to be taped or whether it's going directly on air, you may find the whole experience a little awesome.

Let's assume that you have arrived at the radio station for your interview, which is to be taped and used as part of a program to be released at a later date. Radio station facilities vary from the very sophisticated to the quite basic. When you strip away all the frills, you are going to find yourself sitting in a chair and talking into a microphone while what you say is recorded on audiotape. All the rest is wrapping paper.

Before you reach the microphone, your mind will be filled with a jumble of impressions. Radio stations are busy places. You will feel that everyone in the building except you knows exactly what they are doing there. You will feel a little out of place. With luck, they'll have time to meet you at the switchboard and set about making you feel comfortable, at home, and part of what's going on. They may even have time to find you a cup of coffee.

When the formalities are over and you are ready to go to work, you will find yourself sitting at a small table in a radio "studio." There will be a microphone in front of you and an announcer or "program host" sitting across the table from you ready to ask you questions. You will probably be surprised at how small the room actually is. You may even get the feeling that the interview is being conducted in a telephone booth. Look around. Notice the soundproofing material on the walls. Say something out loud and listen to the sound of your voice. It's a little muffled because of the material on the walls. They want your voice, not its echo, to go onto the recording tape.

The technical aspects of the recording will be attended to by a technician who will be sitting on the other side of a window doing magical things with complex equipment. When you are about ready to begin, the announcer may glance over to the window and receive some form of hand signal from the technician. You may be asked to say a few words of wisdom, but they are just checking the strength of your voice, how the microphone is picking it up, and how it will sound as it goes down on tape. The tabletop in front of you may be covered with green felt to muffle the sound of paper and notes that you have with you, or it may be a piece of plywood scarred by countless cigarettes that have been left to smoulder along its edge while the smoker spoke into the microphone.

It may be all of these things or it may be none of these things, so if you are curious about anything, ask questions. The business of conducting an interview in a radio station is something that's very familiar to the people in the business. It really is all in a day's work for them. They may sometimes forget that people who are not connected with the business find the whole process a little overwhelming. Don't panic. You'll be just fine.

Because the broadcasters are working within a very tight time frame, they may not be able to stop and make you feel at ease by explaining *everything* that's happening or is about to happen. It's not that they don't care, just that they don't have the time. In fairness to your host, you should know that the room in which you are being interviewed is used for many other things during the course of a broadcast day. In a few minutes, for example, someone from the newsroom is going to be sitting in your chair and reading the headlines into the microphone in front of you. The host knows that the newsman is already waiting outside the studio door, pages of yellow paper clutched in his hand, waiting to get in and get set up for his newscast. This adds a certain urgency to the matter of getting on with the interview, but your host doesn't want to put any additional pressure on you, his guest, because he really does want to help you to relax and do the best job you can.

Probably the best way to deal with the situation from *your* point of view is to accept the fact that you don't feel familiar with the surroundings, that the whole experience is new to you. Trust your knowledge and familiarity with your topic. Tell yourself that you are going to have a conversation with just one person, the one sitting across the table from you. Look him in the eye, listen to his questions, and answer those questions as simply as you can in your natural voice. This is not the time to try to sound like Sir Laurence Olivier.

You have something worthwhile to say. That's why you were invited to come to the radio station in the first place. Concentrate on the fact that you are having a conversation with just one other person, the one across the table from you, and that you are talking about something with which you are quite familiar. That's all you really have to remember, because the station staff are there to help you, and things are going to work out very nicely.

If the interview is not being taped, if this is "live" radio, you may feel the pressure just that much more. What happens if you make a mistake? What happens if you have to clear your throat? What happens if you say something you didn't mean to say?

Granted, all of these things could happen. But what if they happened in the course of an ordinary conversation? You'd clear your throat, you'd admit that you'd made a mistake and correct it, and you'd say, "Sorry, that's not what I really meant to say," and then you'd correct that too. It wouldn't be the end of the world.

Because the experience is all very strange to you, you will have a tendency to think about all the things that can go wrong. You want this to go well. You are anxious to do a good job of it, but you are afraid you will have difficulty thinking of the right things to say. All of this is very natural, so when it happens, just remember my father and his first flight on a commercial airline.

My father made his first long airplane flight back in the days of propeller-driven aircraft. He travelled with a friend on the night flight from Edmonton to Montreal on an old four-engined North Star. The friend told me later that my father sat there looking out the window as the sky grew darker. He watched the wing tip flexing up and down with the air currents. He watched the exhaust ring inside the engine cowling glowing red hot. He watched the sparks and flames streaking back from the exhaust ports and he watched the loose rivets dancing in the wings with all the vibration. At which point my father leaned back in his seat, closed his eyes, and was heard to say, "Why should *I* worry? It's not *my* airplane."

If everything at the radio station seems about to fly apart, just say to yourself, "Why should *I* worry? It's not *my* radio station."

You won't have time to familiarize yourself with everything that's going on around you. You won't be there long enough. Most of the people on the staff don't understand everything that's going on around *them*. It may seem simplistic, but concentrate on the fact that you are talking to just one person, the one sitting across the table from you. Granted, he may look a little strange. He may have a mug of coffee in his right hand and a burning cigarette in his left hand and he may have a huge headset clamped over his ears. He may be getting messages from the control room through this headset while you are talking to him, and he may not even be looking at you as you speak. But *he* is the one you are talking to, so just be as natural as you can under the circumstances, difficult as that may seem at the time.

You really are just talking to one person. There may be a lot more listening to you out there somewhere but you are having a one-on-one conversation, and you've had them before and been just fine. You'll be just fine this time too.

If you are a mite anxious about how you are going to sound when this is all over, you may have considered trying a tape-recorder to see what your voice will sound like to others.

In all our discussions about public speaking in all its varied forms, we haven't mentioned tape-recorders as a tool in the preparation process, but it seems logical to consider them when we are talking about radio. Is it a good idea to record what you are going to say and then play it back so that you can hear what you sound like?

There is something very strange about hearing your own voice played back on audiotape. It's an experience that can do more harm than good if you are in any way apprehensive about the business of speaking in public. Most people are surprised at the sound of their own voice when they first hear it played back for them. Many don't even recognize their own voice.

As a rule, when you first hear your voice played back for you, you don't listen to what you are saying, just to the way you sound as you say it. This can be distressing, but only if you dwell on it. Your first brush with the sound of your own voice can throw you off balance.

Concentrate on *what you are saying*, and *how you sound* will usually look after itself.

CHAPTER 15

Look Who's on Television

With community television playing an increasing rôle in our lives, with television news and public affairs programming growing in popularity and technical capability, there is a very real possibility that you will have a chance to appear on television.

Technical change has brought about a new sound to the world of radio, and technical change has brought a new look to the television screen. A news broadcast is no longer the image of talking heads reading the stories to us. Today we are taken to the scene of the accident, to the public forum, and to the high school track meet. The announcer may introduce the stories, but it's the reporter at the scene and the comments of the people at the event that give credibility and impact to the story. The anchorman at the television newsdesk links it all together but it's the people out where the action is that give it the content.

On commercial stations the public affairs programming is drawing the community into the picture, literally. Community programming on the local cable company systems is touching us all. The number of volunteers who give of their time and talent in the production of cable television programs is an indication of the increasing awareness of this way of getting your message to the world around you.

And if you thought your first brush with radio was touched with tension, just wait until you run up against television.

The portability of equipment is more noticeable in the world of television than it is in the radio business. There was a day, and not that long ago either, when television crews had to pack three trucks with gear if they were going to do some filming away from the studio. A television interview usually meant a visit to the television station, but not any more.

Recording something for television away from the studio once meant that the crew used either film or videotape. They still use film or videotape, but the equipment needed to record on the film or tape has changed. At one time, videotape was always two inches wide and the equipment needed to record on the tape fitted not too badly into the back of a truck the size of a moving van. Since the equipment needed so much electricity that there was a danger of plunging the entire neighbourhood into total darkness, the van carried its own source of electrical power. The size and weight of the cameras, the related cables and wires, the lighting equipment plus the recording equipment, made the whole operation just too much for anything but a very special remote broadcast. A remote broadcast was one that originated or was recorded away from the studio.

A simpler technique involved the use of motion picture film. Film worked well, the equipment was smaller and lighter, and the whole operation was far more portable. But the exposed film had to be processed at a film processing laboratory, then viewed to see if the crew had covered everything they set out to shoot. The film would then be edited so that all the essential information was retained and the surplus scenes cut out. A further editing process would trim the film down until it ran for a length of time that fitted into the program for which it was to be used. The use of motion picture film or the complicated videotaping equipment for a remote recording session was deemed necessary to achieve a quality of sound and image that matched the quality of a program produced in the studio.

Fortunately for all concerned, things have changed over the years. Videotape and portable television cameras have improved so much technologically that the crew can now get a quality image down on a narrower videotape and the equipment is a great deal more compact and lighter in weight.

Another of the many advantages of the newer equipment is that of immediate viewing. They don't have to wait for the film to come back from the processing lab to see if they got what they wanted. They just run the videotape back a few feet, peek into a little viewfinder, and run the tape forward to see what has been recorded. No fuss, no muss, no bother. Anyone who has ever exposed a roll of film at a child's birthday party, picked up the prints the next day, and found that there was whipped cream on one corner of the camera lens will appreciate what the instant replay feature of the new equipment can mean.

The size and weight of the video cameras have been reduced to the point where a steady-handed cameraman can leave his tripod in the truck. He can either hold the camera in his hands or, with the aid of a shoulder support, do his shooting as he moves around and produce a picture that is quite acceptable to the average viewer.

News and public affairs programs now use far more footage shot in the field than they used to because of these technological improvements. It makes the news more interesting, believable, and entertaining. It's Show and Tell time on television. Without the pictures it's just Tell Time, which is just radio while you watch the announcer read his script.

The impact of technological change has certainly made a difference to the community cable companies. The huge crews and truckloads of equipment that used to be involved in a filming project away from the studio have been replaced by a two- or three-person crew and a small van carrying all the tools needed to do the job. The technical quality might not meet the high standards of a network production, but from the viewer's point of view the image is quite acceptable.

Because television is getting out of the studio and into the neighbourhood, and because community cable television programming is involving the entire community it serves, more and more people find themselves looking into the lens of a television camera and saying what they've got on their minds. There are obvious differences between making a comment on radio and saying the same thing on television. You can be interviewed over the telephone for radio and the listening audience will never know that you're still in bed in rumpled pyjamas or that your hair is up in curlers.

But there is another difference, perhaps more subtle, and

certainly more significant. A friend of mine does a great deal of work on radio and television in the general area of consumer information. She tells us that people will stop her in the supermarket and say, "I heard your radio item on electric kettles yesterday, and I agree completely with what you had to say." She will be asked to do a piece on children's toys for television and again people will stop her at the supermarket, but this time they say, "I caught your item on television last night and I really liked your hairdo." Yes, there *is* a difference between radio and television.

Somebody once said that television was very much a case of hurry up and wait. You are liable to find that there's a lot of that going around when you first encounter a television camera and the world it can open up for you.

Your roses won first prize at the local horticultural show and the Happy Gardener from the cable station called and asked you to be a guest on his program so that you can tell all those people out there in Television Land how you did it. They asked you to record the half-hour program in advance.

The following Tuesday you arrived at the cable station, you were met at the switchboard, and you've been led to a dark room that seems to be filled with strange pieces of equipment. You've watched the program on your set back home, but it certainly hasn't looked anything like this. There are wires and cables all over the floor and the room looks like a barn. Then, to your amazement, you see a furniture arrangement over against one wall, and it looks familiar. You've seen it before, of course, when you've watched *Flower Time*. There are two comfortable-looking chairs, a coffee table, a piece of rug, and a fireplace which, when you look at it now, appears to be made of cardboard, plywood, and plastic. The whole thing may look a little dusty, and it may even look a little tacky.

Your host or hostess arrives, there are handshakes, and you are invited to be seated in one of the chairs. At this point you may get the feeling that you have become a piece of furniture. A total stranger may walk up and set about clipping something to the lapel of your jacket. It's a small microphone, they will explain, and they may ask you to do something with the wire leading from it, something that

137

hides it and makes it look less obvious to the viewer. Wires now lead away from you and disappear into the gloom. People are moving around out there, shifting pieces of equipment and talking into microphones that are attached to the huge headsets they are wearing. They are having apparently one-sided conversations with people in another part of the building, and if you listen carefully you may realize that the shiny nose they are talking about is yours. In television they carry a lot of clipboards to which they refer at regular intervals.

While all this preparatory work is going on, your host may have a chat with you about the way the program is going to run. This conversation may take place upstairs in the waiting room, in his office, or he may have discussed it with you earlier in a telephone conversation. He will perhaps say something about the format of the show, that it will run for twenty-eight minutes with a two-minute commercial in the middle, for example. He will have a list of questions that he wishes to ask you and he may run through a few of them. This gives you an idea of the sort of information he wants, and you gain confidence as you realize that you are dealing with a comfortable, familiar subject.

Sometimes the interviewer will avoid too much detailed discussion about the questions he has planned. He isn't trying to trick you or catch you off guard. It's more a case of his having confidence in your ability to deal with the subject, and if he goes over the material to be dealt with in too great detail, the questions and answers may sound contrived and rehearsed. He wants this to look like a very relaxed conversation, and if you sound as though you have memorized your answers, he will lose that naturalness.

When they are closer to starting the recording session, bright lights may be turned on over your head. You can't see a thing until your eyes adjust, and even then, what's happening out there in the gloom is even harder to follow. Someone may swing a television set around so that you can see what's being picked up by the cameras. And there you are, in living colour, and it's enough to make your throat go dry.

You are picking up a little more knowledge about what's going on around you when you realize that the television cameras have little red lights on top of them, and the camera whose red light is glowing is the one that is taking the picture you see on the screen. Out there in the darkness people are muttering numbers that don't mean anything to you, and someone else is discussing the backlighting on your hair, whatever that means.

Finally it's down-to-business time and there is a muffled demand for silence out there in the gloom. An apparition kneels down at the edge of light in front of you and flicks his fingers in the direction of the host as he counts backwards, "Ten, nine, eight, seven, six, five seconds to camera..." and then total silence until you hear the familiar theme music coming from a speaker out there somewhere.

The next thing you hear is the voice of the fellow sitting beside you saying, "Good evening, flower lovers of all ages wherever you are, and a warm welcome to *Flower Time* here at your friendly community cable station. Tonight your Happy Gardener is going to talk about the care and feeding of those lovely rose bushes in your garden, and to help us in our conversation, we have that well-known prize-winning rose grower, Herb Stuermer. Hi there, Herb, and welcome to the show. How are you tonight?"

It's actually the middle of the afternoon, which he seems to have forgotten, and if he wants an honest answer about your physical well-being, you think you're about to throw up. You arc quite certain that's not the answer he's expecting. Then you remember that they are *taping* the show for release on an evening later in the week and suddenly the host doesn't seem as dumb as you first thought.

The trick is to try to shut out all that's strange and confusing out there. You are sitting in a comfortable chair and talking to someone who is sitting across a coffee table from you. He's asking questions about a subject that you find familiar, your rose bushes.

That's all you really have to know. The lights, the sound, the cameras, the dark shapes out there moving quietly around the floor may seem a little threatening, but they are out there to help you do what you came to do, and that's talk about your roses. Again, why should *you* worry? It's not *your* television station.

Be yourself. Because you have done well with your roses,

you obviously enjoy them. Relax, and that enthusiasm for your subject will come through. If you have a tickle in your throat, clear it quietly. No need to apologize and make a big thing of it. If you are thirsty and there's a glass of water on the coffee table, have a sip. Concentrate on the person across from you. Listen to the questions. Make sure you've got the question straight in your mind before you answer it. If you're not clear as to what he's asking, get him to repeat it. He's not perfect. Even Barbara Frum doesn't always phrase her questions perfectly the first time she asks them! Better to take the time to be clear than to be quick but confused.

You can move your hands and arms if you feel like it. The little microphone won't fall off. They should have clipped it to a spot that won't be brushed by your arms if you do move them. If the tweed sleeve of your jacket rubs across the microphone they clipped to your lapel, it probably means that they will stop the taping, move your microphone, and then start all over again. If you move around a little before the taping session gets under way, you'll know what movements and gestures feel natural and comfortable.

You can cross your legs if you feel like it. You can even change your position in your chair if you feel like it, but it's a good idea to do your moving when your host is asking a question rather than when you are giving your answer. They'll be switching back and forth from one camera to another for visual variety on the television screen, and when you are talking you can be reasonably sure that one of the cameras is on you and you want to present a nice steady image for the folks at home. Don't try to watch the red lights on the cameras or the image on that television set out there. You are talking to the host, so keep in touch with him and not with the goings-on in the darkness off the set.

They won't be dumb enough to seat you in a swivel chair so that you, with a touch of nervousness, sit there and swivel back and forth during the entire interview. They did that with someone years ago and sold the swivel chair to the junk man the next day.

Keep your eye on your host. Things will be happening out there in the rest of the room but don't worry about them. They'll be fine.

Keep your answers brief. Try to avoid terminology that is very familiar to you but may confuse others. Try to look as though you are having a good time.

The most surprising aspect of the whole experience will be how quickly you hear the host thanking you for coming and apologizing because they have run out of time. You can't believe that it's all over this quickly.

Then the bright lights go off, the studio lights come on, and there are all kinds of nice people telling you what a fine job you did and asking if you can come back in two weeks and talk about the care and feeding of house plants during the winter. Then the second surprising thing happens. You hear your own voice saying you would be delighted. You leave realizing that when you look back on it, the whole thing was a lot of fun and you would *enjoy* doing it again.

Sometime between the day you made your debut on community cable television and the day you go back for your *second* interview, you are liable to see and hear the *first* one you did. You may have some reservations about how your performance looked, so let's talk about that.

If the sound of your own voice on audiotape was distressing, the sight and sound of your image on videotape may throw you into shock, but don't let it upset you. On audiotape you were so caught up with the way you sounded that you didn't listen to what you were saying. On videotape you not only have to contend with the way you sound but with the way you *look* at the same time.

Used properly, there is a great deal to be learned from listening to your own delivery or watching your own performance. People involved in everything from teacher training to golf practice make good use of videotape as a teaching tool, but they use it with a great deal of caution because they know the harm that can be done.

A drafting instructor at an institute of technology asked to be videotaped so that he could see how he looked to his students. He was taken to the television studio and asked to conduct a simple demonstration, which was recorded in colour on videotape. He chose to demonstrate the proper way to unwrap and light a good cigar. Those watching were delighted with the presentation, but when the instructor viewed the playback, he was visibly upset. He left the studio saying he wouldn't sit through an entire lecture by anyone who spoke that badly. It took a considerable amount of counselling to enable him to see himself the way his students and his peers saw him. He was an excellent instructor, but he wasn't ready for the shock of seeing himself on television for the first time.

The simplest things can loom large in your mind when you are watching the playback of your interview. Husbands have been known to turn to their wives and say, "Why didn't you *tell* me I needed a haircut that badly?" This from a fellow who hasn't worried about the length of his hair for forty years.

A university professor looked at his television screen in horror as he saw himself interviewed for the first time. He was wearing his new eyeglasses, the kind that are tinted so that they grow darker in bright light. He watched as the studio lighting caused his glasses to grow darker and darker as the interview progressed. When it was over he remembered nothing of the interview itself, just that he looked like the driver of the getaway car at a bank heist.

If you are going to be on television, dress simply, comfortably, and lightly. Watch for things that might be distracting, either in dress or mannerism. If you stick your finger under your wristwatch strap and flex it back and forth during the entire interview, guess what you are going to notice when you watch it on the screen. Unfortunately, everyone else is likely to notice it too. The simplest things can be most distracting. Remember the actor's diary.

May 16: Dear Diary: Tomorrow night I open on Broadway and my career is launched. The play is a classic. The writing is marvellous and my lines are an actor's dream. The set design is flawless, the lighting is perfect, and in the last act I have a seven-minute soliloquy. I command the stage. The only other person in view is an old man who sits, stage left, making an entry in a ledger with a quill pen and a bottle of ink.

May 17: Dear Diary: He drank the ink.

Not that anybody is going to drink the ink during your appearance on television because you and the host and the station staff will make sure that nothing like that happens.

A television appearance is another form of public speaking, and while you don't get the immediate reaction of an audience, you get the reaction of those around you during the recording session and later, of course, the viewers. They'll let you know that you've done a good job.

A television appearance is exciting, it can be fun, and it can leave you with a very satisfied feeling. It's another example of the nice things that can happen when you accept that invitation to speak. So if the invitation comes along, accept it. You might find that you really enjoy it.

CHAPTER 16

The Way You Look Tonight

If you will be standing up and saying a word or two, it's a good idea to give some thought to how you will *look* as well as to what you will *say*. On the subject of wardrobe, you can sum it all up in two words: *be comfortable*.

Of course it's not quite *that* easy. Being comfortable involves a little bit more than wearing your favourite jeans and a well-worn pair of sneakers. You have to feel comfortable with what you're wearing, true, and that involves not just the way you look, but the way you *feel* about the way you look.

Having said "Be comfortable" to the lady or gentleman who is going to be doing the talking, let's look at all the implications in that simple statement.

You know you will not really wear the same clothes you would wear on a fishing trip even though they are the most relaxing things in your wardrobe. You might wear them, and they might feel just fine as you put them on, but being comfortable with what you wear means that it conforms a little bit, at *least* a little bit, to the standards of our society. You don't wear your "Sun Your Buns In the Bahamas" T-shirt to a job interview.

If this thing is formal and you are expected to wear a tuxedo or, in the case of women, a long dress, someone will have told you this a long time ago. When formal attire isn't mentioned, you are on your own when it comes to planning what you will wear.

Sometimes a letter of invitation will say discreetly that "business suits" are to be worn. They're trying to tell you something. They're saying that while the function isn't formal in the strictest sense of the word, they'd like you to wear a jacket and a pair of pants that match. If it's going to be a fairly serious group, dress accordingly. Your ultimate objective here is to be comfortable, but with all that that implies. You can wear your checkered sports jacket and open-necked golf shirt if you like, but you may not feel very comfortable when you arrive for your talk and find everyone else in the room dressed a little differently. Avoid the feeling that you've got a bone through your nose.

What you should achieve is a choice of clothes that works so well that you don't give them another thought once you put them on and head out the door of your home. *That* is being comfortable with what you are wearing.

Generally speaking, the same ground rules apply to men and women. Make your choice of clothes, check your hair, and put it all together. Then *forget it!* Once you have arrived for your engagement, you shouldn't have to touch anything, adjust anything, or rearrange anything. You should be so comfortable with what you are wearing that you don't give it another thought.

If that sounds difficult, cheer up. The task can be made easier if you start when you are still sorting through your clothes closet.

Keep in mind that if you are going to be saying a few words after a luncheon or dinner, at a meeting at the school auditorium, or in a conference room at the company's sales meeting, it will be warm. The wind may be howling outside the house, but remember that when you reach your destination, you will rarely find a gale blowing through a dining room. There will be warm air, bright lights, and no open windows. Dress according to the room conditions you can reasonably expect. If you are a man and have a favourite three-piece woollen suit that you really like, give it lots of consideration. But if you also have a nice two-piece suit that just came back from the cleaners, and it's light in weight and ready to go, you might be more comfortable wearing that in a hot room. What you want to avoid is a situation in which you try to unbutton your wool vest during the meal so that you'll be a little cooler, at the same time wishing you had left the fool thing back home in your clothes closet.

Most men have a favourite shirt. By all means wear it, as long as you are happy with it. If you have a shirt that you think looks a little nicer but it's a mite snug around the neck and the sleeves are a touch on the short side, forget it. If you are inclined to become tense under the circumstances that you are about to face, keep cool in every way you can. At a time of great turmoil you don't need the choking feeling you get from a shirt collar that's too tight. You can go a little dressy if you wish and wear a shirt with French cuffs. A nice pair of cuff links don't weigh all that much and they don't add to the heat in the room. If you are comfortable with them, then wear them.

Wear clothes that are appropriate to the occasion. If you stop to think about where you will be going and the people who will be there, you won't have any trouble deciding what's appropriate.

You want to be so relaxed about your appearance that you don't give it a second thought once you have arrived for your presentation. If that means getting a haircut, then get a haircut.

A passing thought. Don't ever underestimate the power of a simple shoeshine. Once you have your feet tucked under the tablecloth at the luncheon or dinner, nobody is going to notice your shoes. But there's a deep psychological link between a shoeshine and a feeling of well-being on the part of the shoe wearer that has never been thoroughly explored. A shoeshine makes you *feel* good.

And if you think a shirt collar that's too tight can give you a feeling of discomfort, just consider what a pair of tight shoes can do. Leave the new shoes in the closet for another day. Wear a pair that you know is going to be comfortable. Not only will you be standing in those shoes; you will be walking around in them too. Take your comfort from wherever you can get it, and that can start with your shoes.

If your shoes are too tight, you are liable to have a pained look on your face. The audience may spot the pained look and suffer on your behalf even though they don't know that your problem is an uncomfortable pair of shoes. Not only do *you* want to feel comfortable, you would like your audience to feel comfortable as well.

Helping your audience to feel comfortable is all tied up with the appropriateness of your clothes. If the men in the audience are all wearing jackets, shirts, and ties, and you stand up at the lectern with an open-necked sports shirt and your gold Aztec calendar pendant dangling from the gold chain around your neck, then, sir, guess what the audience is going to notice. They'll remember the sight of the overhead lights glistening on your Aztec calendar as it swung back and forth before their eyes. They may not remember much about what you *said*, but they will remember the flickering light.

Is there a suggestion here that you should look like a clone of everyone in the audience? Certainly not! If you are talking to a group about the need for a little nonconformity in our world today, it might not be a bad idea to introduce a little nonconformity into what you are wearing. A departure from the traditional might be an excellent idea on such an occasion. Putting it another way, it might just be appropriate to wear something out of the ordinary under the circumstances. This is not to contradict what I have been saying. It reinforces it. Wear something that's appropriate to the occasion, and then forget it.

The ladies have the same set of problems, but in the jewelry department it's perhaps a little more pronounced. Pins, pendants, earrings, bracelets, and necklaces all have a trick of catching the light. They're designed that way. When you stand up at a head table, you can count on the fact that there will be lots of light. Check your choice of jewelry. You want your audience to notice you and hear what you have to say. You don't want them to be distracted by the flash of light from a pair of earrings that have reflected the overhead lights at just the wrong moment. You are something that is to be looked at and *listened* to, not something dangling from the roof and rotating in the middle of the dance floor at a discotheque.

A lady invited to appear on television might very profitably spend some extra time considering hair styles, makeup, and accessories. There are highly competent women doing a very professional job on our television screens these days. What they wear, how they have their hair styled, and the way they accessorize their wardrobes are conscious choices made to reinforce their image of competency, not distract from it.

As an individual you know what works well for you when it comes to appearance. You know when you feel comfortable with your choice of clothes. But we can all learn from others, and if you are curious as to what might be the very best for you, why not check out the women on your television screen over a period of days or a week? See what works best for them, and see if there's anything that you might apply to your situation. It could be a very interesting and valuable learning experience. It doesn't take much time, the hours are good, and you can't beat the tuition fees.

Feeling comfortable is the sum of many little things, and perhaps the smallest of these can be a button. If you've made your choice of clothes, take a minute or two well in advance of the moment you start to put them on. Is there a button missing from the top of your favourite shirt or loose on the front of your favourite blazer? It may need a little help with a needle and thread, which is no problem if you have lots of time. If it's loose, the Button Demon is going to cause it to come off in your fingers when you are dressing with just minutes to spare.

Is there a gravy spot in the middle of your necktie? You can't send it to the cleaners five minutes before you head out the front door. Trying to sponge it off may not do much good for the spot, but it can certainly do interesting things to your blood pressure.

If you are going to wear a particular set of cuff links or earrings, make sure there are two of them before you start to put them on. You don't need the pressure of a lost earring when you have other things on your mind.

Adopt a little of the Boy Scout philosophy: Be Prepared.

Murphy's First Law of Nervous Tension states that if your shoelace is going to break, it will always break at a time when you can least afford the nuisance. Murphy's Second Law of Nervous Tension states that when your shoelace breaks, it will always break at a time and place where it's impossible to find a replacement.

Details, true, and picky ones at that. But peace of mind and personal composure can begin with knowing that all the details have been attended to. Having done that, you can then concentrate on the more important matters close at hand.

CHAPTER 17
Spicing Up the Sauce

When you have been asked to say a few words, you are not necessarily limited to *just* words.

Any presentation can be spiced up a little if the person doing the presenting works in something a little different, if there is a touch of freshness to the thing. It can be exciting to find a fresh and original approach to the presentation of material that has been cranked out in the same way time after time in the past.

Try a little imagination as you plan your presentation. If it involves turning off all the lights and showing a few slides, it may help to ease your nervous tension if you realize that you will be able to work in the dark for a little while.

A fellow was once asked to present a safety lecture to a group of sewer construction foremen at a city safety seminar. He had accepted before he realized all the implications in the invitation. He didn't know a thing about underground construction, and there were going to be people at the seminar who had years of experience at open-cut trenching and deep-tunnel work. He had a certain amount of freedom as to topic, just as long as it pertained to safety and sewer construction within a city.

He used his imagination and decided to present the foremen with a lecture on traffic control and pedestrian safety around construction projects. Without doubt this was certainly a worthwhile topic. Hard to make interesting, true, but very worthwhile if he could bring it off.

You have been faced with the situation yourself. You are driving blithely along a city street when suddenly you encounter a set of barricades that are supposed to guide you safely around a trenching operation. There may even be a flagman on the job to make sure you slow down and swing well clear of the construction crew.

But the barricades are often anything but helpful in letting you know where you should go. The flagman doesn't help much either. All too often he's the nitwit on the crew that the foreman would like to get out of the way for the day. The foreman gives him a red flag nailed to the end of an old broom handle and sends him half a block back up the street and tells him to direct traffic.

Our friend felt that the need for improvement of traffic control around construction sites was important. But how was he, an outsider, to gain the confidence of his audience and then talk to them about the most effective ways to handle traffic around their ditching operations?

He borrowed a friend's home movie camera, he wangled enough money out of petty cash to buy three rolls of film, and he borrowed a car and driver for an afternoon. They drove around the city and, with his helper at the wheel, our speaker pointed his camera out the windshield of the car and shot film footage of what the motorist saw as he approached a variety of ditching operations.

The day of his presentation he was introduced to the foremen assembled at the meeting, he quickly told them what he hoped to accomplish, and then he invited them to go for a drive around the city with him without ever leaving the comfort of the room. He suggested to them that, with luck, by the time they got back from their trip around the city they would be convinced that there might be a little room for improvement in the handling of traffic and the barricading of construction projects. Then he showed his film. The foremen, for the first time in their lives, looked out the windshield of a car and *saw* what their jobs looked like to a passing motorist.

Our friend, having caught their attention and their imaginations, went on to discuss a variety of ways in which they could improve their traffic control. He presented the material along the lines that they, the foremen, could improve the safety and efficiency of their projects and at the same time fulfill a vital public relations rôle as far as handling passing traffic was concerned.

A tough topic mixed with a little imagination produced a winning formula. You can, without too much difficulty, think of ways to give your talk an edge. But be careful. Don't sell the edge.

You've seen that happen in television commercials. You are entranced with the cleverness of some of the commercials, but when they are over you can't remember the name of the product or the sponsor. They put so much edge in some of the commercials that all you remember is the edge, and that's not exactly what the sponsor had in mind.

Use a little imagination in your presentation, but don't let the unique presentation obscure the message.

It always helps to keep your expected audience in mind as you do your imagining. What will arouse their interest and keep them listening?

A sales engineer with the marketing department of a cement company faced a difficult challenge. He had been invited to make a presentation at a training seminar for the staff of a local concrete plant. He had been asked to demonstrate the variation in the amount of water it takes to saturate a given volume of sand and gravel when the size of the particles varies from one sample to another. As if that weren't bad enough, he then learned that the night of the seminar the television networks were carrying a playoff game in the Stanley Cup finals. His audience might be there because the boss had told them to be there, but their minds were going to be somewhere else.

He brought with him in his briefcase two clear glass tumblers, a bag of marbles, and a bottle of white sand. When it was his turn to talk to the plant crew on the night in question, he started into his topic without a trace of a smile. As he explained what he hoped to demonstrate, he assembled his glasses, his marbles, and his sand on the table in front of him. He said that he would fill one glass with marbles and the other with sand. He would then fill the glasses with fluid, letting it flow down into the air spaces between the particles. He would then drain off the fluid and measure it to see if there was a difference between the amounts held by the two glasses. Would it take more fluid to fill the air spaces in the glass with the marbles or the glass with the sand? His audience had something to look at as he talked, and they watched with growing interest as he poured the marbles into the first glass and the sand into the second.

David Ogilvy claims that the secret of a successful television commercial is to pose a problem, suggest a solution, and then follow it up with a believable demonstration. Our friend was following this three-step procedure with his presentation to the plant crew.

Then, feigning great distress, he told his audience that he had forgotten to bring any fluid. With a shrug, he said that no sacrifice was too great for such an important demonstration. He reached back into his briefcase and produced a bottle of Scotch whiskey.

Again, without a trace of a smile or a word of explanation, he carefully filled each glass to the brim with "fluid" and went on with his experiment. Those men might have been a little indifferent *before* he produced that bottle of Scotch, but he had their undivided attention from that moment on. He never did tell them whether it was real Scotch or cold tea, and when they went home that night the only person who really knew was the demonstrator.

A tray filled with 35mm slides can be an invaluable aid to bringing a lecture to life. But you, in turn, can bring the *slides* to life with a little imagination built into your presentation.

You've been asked to bring some of your slides with you when you come to the next meeting of your mixed bridge club so that you might show the group what a great time you had on your fly-in fishing trip to that northern bush camp. Some of the audience might be fascinated, but you are going to have trouble with the rest. Let's look at a way to get everyone on your side.

Pick out your fishing trip slides, of course, but let's give a little thought to the four or five slides that you might just drop in at the head end of the slide tray. Prowl around your slide collection and see what you find. There's one of the international airport, the one you took when you flew south for your vacation and arrived at the airport good and early.

Put it to one side. You might be able to use it.

Have you got any pictures taken from the top of the Empire State Building in New York? Great. Pick one of them and put it to one side. How about the one you took out the windshield of the car when you were being driven along a gravel road that was so dusty you could barely see the hood ornament? You can use that one too. How about that one of the taxi parked on the side street in Mexico, the taxi that made a Model A Ford look like a Ferrari? That'll do too!

Arrange them in order at the beginning of your slide tray. First the shot of the international airport. Then the shot of the Mexican taxi. The picture of the dusty road can go in next, and then the shot from the top of the Empire State Building. Then why not drop in the slide you took of the girl at the beach last summer, the one who looked like a *Playboy* centrefold? You told your wife that you were photographing the sailboat in the background when she just happened to walk in front of the camera.

When you are ready to make your pitch to the bridge club, turn off the room lights, put the first slide on the screen, and say something about, "Our party left on our great adventure from the local international airport, and in minutes, it seemed, our speedy jet was coming in for a landing on the paved runways of the Mosquito Narrows International Airport in the Northwest Territories. Waiting for us when we cleared customs and gathered our gear was the luxury limousine that had been chartered to take us to our water transportation. (Picture of Mexican taxi)

"Our skillful driver made his way out onto the multi-laned freeway (shot of dusty road) and before we knew it, we were in beautiful downtown Mosquito Narrows. To get our bearings, we climbed to the top of the highest structure in town, the local water tower, and gazed down at the humble and primitive village below us. (Slide of New York from the Empire State Building)

"The next morning we were up bright and early and ready for the canoe trip to our campsite. As we made our way to the edge of the river and our canoes, we were joined by our faithful guide. (Shot of lady bather)"

By now your audience is a little off balance and waiting to find out what surprise you will play on them with the next slide. Your next slide is the first one in the series of your fishing trip, but you've certainly got their attention.

Rather than plunging right into the fishing trip pictures, you have eased your audience into them gently. With a touch of luck you've put your little group at ease and lifted the whole thing out of the ritual of "my holiday slides" that we've seen so often. There's no limit to the varieties of approach you can take to your presentation, except perhaps the limits of good taste and time.

If you want to test your audience's awareness by switching your commentary around a little so that it doesn't quite match the slides, give them a chance to catch up. They may, at first, think that you've got a slide in the wrong place. Give them some time to realize that you're all having a laugh together, but don't underscore the point with words. Let them do a little work, and don't talk down to them.

A pitch to the staff at a sales meeting can take on a new life if you let your imagination wander as you consider how you will make your presentation. Think about illustrating your talk with slides or graphics of some sort. There's no law that says you have to use just *words*. Seventy-six bar charts in a variety of colors isn't the answer, either. You want a fresh approach, an original one.

A Sunday school teacher who was rather good at sleight of hand used to get the attention of his class of Grade Three boys by doing one or two simple magic tricks while he was talking to them. He didn't draw attention to what his hands were doing. In fact, he did the very opposite. He discussed what he was going to talk about that morning, and the boys sat, fascinated, watching his hands while he spoke to them. They weren't just fascinated. They were quiet. Then, having caught their attention and calmed them down, he went on about the business at hand.

The sleight of hand worked with the small group of boys. It wouldn't have worked at all with a larger group. They wouldn't have been able to see what he was doing. Tailor your presentation to the size of your audience.

When you are asked to make a presentation, think about spicing up your sauce a little. A touch of the right spice can work wonders with a sauce that in turn can make the whole meal memorable.

CHAPTER 18

Don't be Afraid to Make it Person-to-Person

We have been discussing the business of public speaking from the point of view of someone who knows what to say but isn't quite sure of the best way to say it.

We have assumed that you have experience or knowledge or beliefs that you have been asked to discuss with other people, and then gone on from there. But there will be those who rise from their chairs at this point and ask about the times you are asked to speak when you *don't* have any particular background that makes you a logical choice. What about the time you were asked to thank the ladies who had prepared the lunch for the Home and School meeting? What about the time you were asked to say a few words at Old Charlie's retirement party? What about the time you were asked to propose a toast to the absent members at your club meeting?

In those cases, you might argue, you were asked to say something but you *didn't* have any particular experience or knowledge or beliefs that you were asked to discuss. What are you supposed to do in cases like these?

The point was made earlier that you were asked to speak because, in somebody's mind, you had something to say. It's just as true to say that you were asked to say a few words at Old Charlie's retirement party because, in somebody's mind, you had something to say.

When you were asked to say a few words of thanks to the ladies who had worked in the kitchen or to propose a toast to the bride at a wedding, you were asked because it was felt that you had something worthwhile to say. Take another look at these invitations before you decline. It's an honour to be asked to toast the bride or bid Old Charlie farewell. You should be proud of the fact that you were asked.

When an invitation like this comes along, you may have lots of time to prepare your remarks or you may have just enough time to brush the crumbs from your lap, stand up, and ask the ladies in the kitchen if they would mind stepping into the room for a minute.

Let's look at the no-warning situation, and let's assume that you *have* been asked to thank the ladies who prepared the after-meeting lunch for the Home and School meeting. You were sitting there finishing your coffee when this year's president of the Association came over and asked you to thank the people who had worked in the kitchen. By the time you got your tongue organized to say you *wouldn't* do it, the president was on his way back to his table, thanking you for agreeing to do it, and saying that he knew he could always count on you to come through when the chips were down. You can't back out now, so what do you do?

Let's assume you have a couple of minutes before the coffee cups are all cleared away. Why not reach for a paper serviette, get out your ballpoint pen, and make a note or two?

How many people are at the meeting enjoying their coffee and snack? How many worked in the kitchen? As Winston Churchill put it, never was so much owed by so many to so few. If you come up with something like that, fine, but what else can you say?

It's time to put the thing on a personal basis. How would *you* like to have spent the evening in a hot kitchen? Right now they are out there up to their elbows in soapsuds doing the dishes. Everybody else came to hear the guest speaker but as always there are a few in the crowd who are willing to give of their time and their talents that the rest of the group might have a pleasant end to a stimulating evening. You have been asked to say thanks to those few. That's all you have to do, say thanks, but you should expand on that a *little*.

You want them to know that not just yourself, but everyone in the room, appreciates the fact that they took an evening when they might have been sitting down listening to a first-class speaker and spent it in a hot kitchen fiddling around with coffee urns, setting out cakes and cookies, and just generally working hard so that others could thoroughly enjoy their evening. You want them to know that what they have done has *not* gone unnoticed, and it certainly *is* appreciated.

If you take just a minute to think about what these ladies have contributed and what it would have been like if they had *not* been there in the kitchen, you won't have too much trouble coming up with something nice to say. End it with an expression of your appreciation, clap your hands together to show that appreciation, and the next thing you know everyone in the room is doing the same thing because you said it for them all. The ladies from the kitchen are smiling too because their contribution to the evening has not gone unnoticed or unthanked.

You are asked to say a few words at Old Charlie's retirement party because you have something to say. You may not realize that you have something to say, but don't fret. It's going to come to you with a little thought.

You have worked next to Charlie since you joined the firm, and he had been on the staff for a good many years at that time. He won't be in on Monday morning. He's retiring at the end of the week and there's to be this little do in the lunchroom after work on Friday. The boss will make the presentation, but you have been asked to pass on the thoughts of the rest of the staff because you have worked with Charlie over the years and in the eyes of the staff you two are old friends.

All of which is fine, but what are you going to say?

You've got until Friday afternoon to work on it, but don't put it off until the last minute. Write down a few of the things you remember about Charlie as the week progresses. You don't want to embarrass the man in any way but you want him to know that you certainly have been aware of his presence over the years. As the days go by you will find that your list of memories about Old Charlie has grown, and grown nicely. There were the little things that only you might be aware of.

Charlie used to come to work with socks that didn't match during the winter months and he blamed it on the dark mornings, claiming that he couldn't see what he was pulling out of his sock drawer from the middle of November until the end of March.

Then there was the time that Charlie enrolled in the memory-development course to help his on-the-job performance rating. On the following Friday afternoon he rode home with the car pool as usual. Charlie had to take the bus back downtown Friday night to pick up the car he had driven to work that morning so he could collect the birthday cake for his wife on the way home from the office. But he got a great mark on the final exam of the memory-development course, didn't he?

Then there was the winter day when your wife was in the recovery room after surgery, and Charlie came over to your desk and didn't say a word. He just picked up all your work, moved it to his desk, got your hat and coat down and pushed them in your direction, and *then* he said, "Why don't you scram? There's somewhere else you should be right now."

He didn't wait for an answer. He just turned around and went back to work. Charlie didn't use many words at the best of times, and that wasn't the best of times. Probably there wasn't anyone else in the office who had seen Charlie from quite that angle.

If you think ahead to Monday morning, you might find you're feeling a twinge or two as you think about what it will be like *without* Charlie. He's been around for so long he had become like a piece of furniture that was *always* going to be around. And while you're at it, you might consider for a moment or two just how *Charlie's* going to feel on Monday morning.

There's your list, and there's your farewell to Old Charlie. Talk about him as a real person. Treat him as a real person. Don't be afraid to tell him that you are going to miss him, and don't be afraid to tell him that you hope he misses you a little bit too.

A touch of honest emotion isn't going to do you any harm.

As the week moves along, keep your list handy. You may think of something to add to it, even in the middle of the night. But be careful about those flashes of inspiration that come in the wee small hours of the night.

A friend of mine was an ardent short story writer, and he believed firmly in the stroke of inspiration that comes with the things that go bump in the night. He kept a pad and pencil on his bedside table, the better to record these insights when they rose from deep in his subconscious. He tells of the night he awoke with the perfect plan for a *New Yorker* magazine short story crisp and clear in his mind. He reached for his pencil and pad of paper and wrote down one word which, he knew, would bring the whole plot back to mind in the morning. He went back to sleep and awoke the next morning remembering his adventure of the night before. He reached for the pad upon which was the key to his *New Yorker* masterpiece, and he stared in disbelief at the word he had written during the night.

"Phlarb!"

To this day he can't remember what the idea was all about, but he certainly wishes he had gone into a little more detail in the middle of the night.

You may be asked to propose a toast or ask the blessing before a meal. You will be chosen because somebody felt that you have something to say. You may think that you haven't a *thing* to say, but look inside yourself and you will find something there if you just let your honest emotions have a chance to move forward. In many instances it's not so much that you don't have anything to say, just that you feel awkward saying it out loud.

You look across the top of your wine glass at the young lady who has just been married. You would like to tell her that seeing her tonight, remembering her as a little kid trying to learn how to catch a baseball with her eyes open so her big brother wouldn't be embarrassed, has made you very much aware of the passage of time. You're a little choked up is what you are, and you'd like to tell her that you are proud of the way she has grown up, and that you think the fellow who married her is a very lucky young man, and that you wish that life could always be as exciting and happy as it is for her that night but you know it isn't going to be. But you know too that she has the "stuff" to cope with the bad times. You would like to say all these things to her, but you feel awkward. You are getting into your personal emotions and it's cutting a little close to the bone, too close for comfort.

But if you'd really like to say those things, why don't you? Just because they come from the heart doesn't mean that you should keep them there.

There will be lots of occasions when you will be asked to say a few words in public, occasions when you think that you really have nothing to say. But almost without fail you *do* have something to say. You just haven't been looking in the right place.

Look again. You'll find it.

CHAPTER 19

Thanks for the Memories

There are a great many benefits to be derived from a little exposure to public speaking, not the least of which can be a very selfish one. You get a chance to gather some marvellous memories.

We have poked fun at quite a few aspects of the public speaking thing, aspects that range from the terrors of stage fright, through the problem of over-exposure to the house wine, and on to the microphone that falls off the stand and drops to the floor at your feet. What we haven't talked about are the interesting people whom you meet, the experiences you have a chance to enjoy, and the warm bank of memories that can build up if you just give it a chance.

There was the night of the mathematics teachers' dinner, for example. The challenge had come in the form of an invitation to do an after-dinner thing for the wind-up banquet of a Mathematics Council meeting. The *real* challenge arose from a long-standing hang-up about mathematics. A high school teacher had supplied three years of exposure to algebra and trigonometry with precious little retention. I had this nagging feeling that if I were so bold as to address a conference of mathematics teachers, I would be found out and my old teacher would come down from heaven and flunk me retroactively in Algebra 30.

But accept we did, and approached the night with great apprehension and many misgivings. They didn't have a formal head table that night, just a separate table set off to one side that had been reserved for those involved in the evening's proceedings. There was a floor-stand with a microphone on it in one corner of the room.

There we sat, my wife and I, along with the chairman for the night and the Program Chairman for the Mathematics Council conference. The Program Chairman was the one who had extended the original invitation. During the meal the conversation touched on many things, none of them of great worldly consequence. Then the Program Chairman mentioned that they were delighted with their choice of hotel for the conference. He extolled the virtues of the various meeting rooms, the friendliness of the staff, and the quality of the meals.

"Of course," he went on, "the rooms are a little expensive for schoolteachers, in that they're asking $47.50 a night for double occupancy. It's not too bad, though," he continued. "If a couple of the teachers double up and split the cost of the room, $28.50 a night isn't bad." And I sat there thinking that if the Program Chairman for a mathematics conference hadn't mastered long division, what was *I* worried about?

An invitation to speak to the same group came up two years later, and during the conversation over lunch, I mentioned this little bit of business that had cropped up at the earlier meeting. I was told that while *that* had been embarrassing enough, what had happened the following year was even worse.

The Program Committee had made arrangements with another hotel in another city for a special rate for delegates to the Math Council meeting. After long hours of negotiation with the hotel management, they had hammered out a special rate of $48.50 per night, double occupancy, for all delegates to the conference. The trick was that you had to identify yourself as a delegate to the Math Council conference when you checked in at the hotel in order to qualify for the special rate. If you *failed to* identify yourself as a delegate to the Mathematics Council conference you didn't get the $48.50 rate, you had to pay the regular double-occupancy weekend rate of $45.00 a night!

Looking back it would appear that a great many of the delightful memories hinge around meetings with school-teachers, but it probably just seems that way. There was, though, that interesting luncheon at a country town when the teachers from that district were holding their annual Professional Development day. All classes in the district had been cancelled. The teachers from all the outlying schools had gathered at the central high school and were being treated to a day of heavy lectures and seminars on their professional upgrading. I had been asked to talk to them following their noon meal, before their afternoon sessions got underway.

The food for the luncheon was to be supplied by the local Ballet Mothers as a fund-raising venture. The Ballet Mothers had outdone themselves. The buffet luncheon prepared for the teachers was a sight to behold and a sensation to eat. In fact it was such a sensation that the first batch of teachers to go past the buffet tables loaded their plates to such an extent that the Ballet Mothers ran out of food with roughly a hundred teachers still to be fed.

Confusion reigned supreme, and there is the marvellous memory of the chairman for the day standing up to introduce the luncheon speaker and prefacing her remarks with the announcement that an emergency order had been telephoned in to the local Chinese food take-out restaurant, and that it would be served as soon as it arrived.

Halfway through the luncheon address the emergency food supply *did* arrive. The Ballet Mothers didn't have any trouble identifying those who hadn't been fed. Their stomachs were rumbling so loudly that it sounded as though Sir Neville Marriner was conducting a rehearsal of the Academy of St. Martin in the Fields.

It's a little tricky holding the attention of an audience when people are wandering up and down the aisles saying, "Who's for chicken chow mein?" A less urbane audience might have exhibited some restiveness, but not this group. It was just one of those things which must be taken in stride, even by the speaker. You remember the natural warmth of people like that.

Then there was the night when, just nicely into the after-dinner address, a telephone immediately behind the head table began to ring. We are a society trained to answer a ringing telephone, but nobody at the head table could find the thing, and they tried. I didn't feel that I should leave the lectern and help, but I was tempted.

While this may not seem to be the most hilarious situation in which a speaker could find himself, when I think about it there is this visual image that comes to mind. It's the image of the headwaiter, dressed in white tie and tails. He had stationed himself at the back of the dining room, lord of all he surveyed. When the telephone started to ring, he started to run. There's something about a person in white tie and tails sprinting around the perimeter of a dining room that can't help but make you laugh. We can only conclude that the telephone call was from his bookie.

Another night, at a CPR hotel that must forever remain nameless, contributed a priceless memory for the collection. It was before the hotel had been updated and the elevators were still handled by operators. The dinner was over, the after-dinner address was over, and the mezzanine floor was jammed with people heading up to their rooms to freshen up before they returned to the dining room for an evening of dancing and socializing.

The elevators were slow in arriving, and there was a certain testiness to the crowd. An elevator stopped, the doors opened, and before anyone had a chance to move towards it the young lady operating the car took two paces forward, and with her hands at her side and her eyes looking straight ahead she said, "Cuckoo!" She took two paces backwards, the elevator doors closed, and she was gone. The roar of laughter that swept that mezzanine floor is a sound to be remembered.

Another night found us in Fort McMurray, the heart of the oil sands development in Northern Alberta. The occasion was the first annual dinner of the Fort McMurray Burns Club. We were honouring Robert Burns with all the trappings that go with such an event. Pipers, dancers, haggis, and the toast to the Immortal Memory of Robert Burns. That toast was my reason for being there.

The oil sands development was just getting under way and the population of Fort McMurray had exploded. There were people moving to the town from all over the world. In the midst of all this industrial activity, one of the long-time residents of Fort McMurray, Alex Haxton, had organized the Burns Club and planned the evening. It was the largest single social event held in Fort McMurray up to that time.

After the formal dinner, which included everything a Burns Supper should have, including the piping in of the haggis, the address to the haggis, and the toast to the Immortal Memory, it was agreed by one and all that this was the biggest thing to hit Fort McMurray since Peter Pond had patched his canoes with oily sand from the banks of the Athabasca River.

When the formalities had been dispensed with we moved to smaller tables for the social portion of the evening. The people at our table formed a rather interesting group. There were Alex and Alice Haxton to start with, Scots to the core. Next to them sat Sue and Bob Theeker. Bob, born in Yorkshire, had been an engineer on an ocean liner and, while docked in Hong Kong, he had wooed and won a local beauty of Chinese descent. Bob was employed by the firm building the extraction plant and Sue did what she could to cope with the cold weather and the general lack of Chinese culture in the area.

Next to the Theekers sat Sally and Baptiste Tootoo. Sally was a Jewish sociologist from Montreal who had moved to the north to teach and train the native population. She contended that native people can fill any responsible job in a technological society. She had married Baptiste, an Eskimo who had worked his way up to a supervisory position at the oil sands plant.

There was the Reverend Peter Harris, the local Anglican priest. He had been a song-and-dance man on the London stage until a motorcycle accident brought his career to a halt. He had immigrated to Canada with his wife, one of the dancers in the chorus line. He had made a small fortune growing grass seed on a farm in Northern Alberta, retired, entered an Anglican seminary, and was at the time ministering to his flock in Fort McMurray.

You can't help but pile up memories when you spend an evening with a group like that.

Later that same evening, as I sat next to Alex Haxton, the conversation swung to other Burns suppers in other circumstances. The soft Scots accent of Alex Haxton still comes to mind as he recalled his most memorable Burns Supper. He had been part of the crew of an RAF Wellington bomber that had been shot down over the Mediterranean Sea during World War II. The survivors had been picked up and transported to a prisoner-of-war camp in Italy. Memory brings back the sound of the piper and the dancers in the background, but it also brings back the sound of a voice lost in thought in that Fort McMurray hotel dining room.

Alex Haxton was remembering his days in the prisoner-of-war camp, of scrounging and saving bits of fruit and raisins from Red Cross packages. He recalled scrounging bits of meat and sausage from the meal trays. The fruit and raisins went into a crock and became a somewhat refreshing batch of homebrew over a period of time. The bits of meat went into a sausage casing and became a haggis. Listening to that voice in that northern community on a cold January night telling of the Burns Supper held in the Italian prisoner-of-war camp with the address to the haggis, the toast to the Immortal Memory with the homebrew, and the lonely voices singing the songs of home... that's the stuff that memories are made of.

There was another night in another city when the chairman for the evening decided, in his infinite wisdom, that the diners had been sitting long enough by the time they had cleared away the dessert. He stood up and told the assembled guests that there would be a fifteen-minute recess before he introduced the guest speaker. Have you any idea what it feels like to be the after-dinner speaker who sits there and watches four hundred and fifty people stand up and walk out of the room?

They all came back, and they sat down and listened. But there's always the memory of the fire drill that took place fifteen minutes earlier.

There are a great many interesting people and a great many fascinating experiences tucked away in the memory bank, none of which would be there if the invitation to say a few words hadn't been accepted. In the words of Richard Needham of the Toronto *Globe and Mail*, "Never put off until tomorrow what you can do today. You may find you like it, and then you can do it again tomorrow."

And how do you sum it all up—the people, the places, the experiences? I can't think of a better way than the four words Bob Hope uses to wind up his appearances on stage, screen, and radio.

Thanks for the memories.

Just Remember

1. Don't reject an invitation to participate in a program without giving it a little thought.

2. Don't take the little details for granted. An ounce of checking can be worth more than a whole bottle of antacid tablets if things are likely to be overlooked.

3. Don't preface anything by saying, "That reminds me of a story."

4. Don't fret unduly about the sound of your voice. If you have done a good job of sorting out what you want to say, the way you sound when you are saying it will look after itself.

5. Don't try to imitate someone else's style. Let Bill Cosby do it *his* way, and you do it *your* way.

6. Don't use technical terms or technical language any more than is absolutely necessary.

7. Don't use ethnic jokes to try to lighten things up, but don't be afraid to draw on your own ethnic background as a source of material.

8. Don't talk down to your audience. Treat them with respect and they will respond in kind.

9. Don't underestimate the power of the wine glass. Like a clove of garlic, a little goes a long way.

10. Don't try to talk to the entire listening audience in the course of a conversation on radio or television. Talk to the one person closest to you, and if anyone else is listening, they will follow along.

11. Don't let the mechanics of television throw you. The equipment may be complex, but your comments don't necessarily have to match.

To Speak Effectively in Public

1. Do remember that when you are asked to participate in a program of any kind it is because somebody thinks you have something to contribute.

2. Do take the time to establish clearly what is expected of you.

3. Do start your preparation in lots of time.

4. Do concentrate on your opening. A good impression goes a long way.

5. Do try to establish a rapport with your listeners as soon as you can.

6. Do give your audience a chance to breathe once in a while. Ease back on the heavy stuff with something a little lighter and brighter; then you can go for the throat again.

7. Do look for a strong way to close. Leave them on a high note, but without any doubt that you have finished.

8. Do look at your audience as much as you can, and talk *to* them. They are on your side.

9. Keep it simple!

10. Do remember that the essence of humour is in the treatment, not in the topic.

11. Do take the time to familiarize yourself with any piece of equipment you will be using, be it a microphone, a lectern, or a projector.

12. Do remember that stage fright isn't fatal, and that you can do a great deal to minimize its effects.

13. Do give a little thought to what you wear. The operative word is comfort, with all that that implies.

14. Do try to present your material in a fresh way. Your listeners will love you for it.

15. Do treasure your memories!